© **Copyright Bibble and Beans Books, LLC 2024 - All rights reserved.**

The content within this book may not be reproduced, duplicated or transmitted without direct written permission from the author or the publisher.

Under no circumstances will any blame or legal responsibility be held against the publisher, or author, for any damages, reparation, or monetary loss due to the information contained within this book. Either directly or indirectly. You are responsible for your own choices, actions, and results.

Legal Notice:

This book is copyright protected. This book is only for personal use. You cannot amend, distribute, sell, use, quote or paraphrase any part, of the content within this book, without the consent of the author or publisher.

Disclaimer Notice:

Please note the information contained within this document is for educational and entertainment purposes only. All effort has been expended to present accurate, up-to-date, and reliable, complete information. No warranties of any kind are declared or implied. Readers acknowledge that the author is not engaging in the rendering of legal, financial, medical or professional advice. The content within this book has been derived from various sources. Please consult a licensed professional before attempting any techniques outlined in this book.

By reading this document, the reader agrees that under no circumstances is the author responsible for any losses, direct or indirect, which are incurred as a result of the use of the information contained within this document, including, but not limited to, — errors, omissions, or inaccuracies.

CONTENTS

Introduction	7
CHAPTER 1	11
Understanding ADHD	11
The ADHD Brain	12
Different Brains	14
Diagnosis Journey	15
Impact on Family	16
The Emotional Journey of Parenting a Child with ADHD	18
ADHD and Family Dynamics: Navigating Sibling Relationships	22
Building a Supportive Home Environment for Neurodiversity	25
2. THE ALCHEMY OF COMMUNICATION: TRANSFORMING UNDERSTANDING INTO ACTION	31
Mastering Empathetic Listening to Understand Your Child	32
Dialogue Tools That Reduce Conflict and Build Trust	38
Encouraging Your Child to Express Emotions Constructively	42
Navigating School Meetings: Advocacy and Collaboration	47
3. CRAFTING CALM IN THE CHAOS	53
The Importance of Routine for Children with ADHD	53
Flexible Scheduling: Adapting to the Unpredictable	60

Organizational Systems That Empower
Children with ADHD 64
Balancing Structure with Spontaneity: Family
Time Redefined 68

4. EMBRACING THE SPECTRUM: A
STRENGTH-BASED APPROACH TO ADHD 73
Highlighting Strengths: A New Perspective
on ADHD 74
Activities That Showcase Your Child's Unique
Abilities 78
Fostering a Growth Mindset in Your
Neurodiverse Child 82
Neurodiversity and Identity: Conversations
with Your Child 84

5. TRANSFORMING TURMOIL INTO
TRANQUILITY 89
Understanding the Triggers of Explosive
Behavior 90
Post-Meltdown Conversations: Healing and
Learning 100
Preventing Explosive Behavior Through
Predictive Planning 105

6. STEERING THROUGH EMOTIONAL SKIES:
SELF-REGULATION IN CHILDREN
WITH ADHD 113
Self-Regulation Skills for Different Ages and
Stages 113
Mindfulness and Meditation Techniques for
Focus 120
Using Play to Enhance Self-Control and
Attention 123
Tailoring Educational Content to Maintain
Focus 126

7. CULTIVATING EMOTIONAL
INTELLIGENCE IN ADHD 129
Emotional Literacy: Teaching Kids to Name
Their Feelings 130
Strategies for Developing Emotional
Regulation 137

Building Resilience Through Problem-Solving Skills ... 142
Celebrating Emotional Milestones and Resilience ... 145

8. POSITIVE DISCIPLINE AND THE ART OF REINFORCEMENT ... 151
Understanding the Role of Positive Reinforcement ... 152
Setting Boundaries and Expectations with Empathy ... 158
The Power of Natural Consequences ... 162
Creative Solutions for Common Behavioral Challenges ... 167

9. NURTURING THE SEED OF ACADEMIC SUCCESS IN THE ADHD CLASSROOM ... 175
Collaborating with Teachers for an ADHD-friendly Classroom ... 176
IEPs and 504 Plans: Advocacy and Implementation ... 181
Homework Strategies That Work for ADHD ... 184
Encouraging Lifelong Learning and Curiosity ... 188

10. FOSTERING SOCIAL FLOURISHING FOR CHILDREN WITH ADHD ... 191
Coaching Your Child on Friendship Skills ... 191
Navigating Playdates and Social Gatherings ... 197
Dealing with Bullying and Social Challenges ... 201
Fostering Empathy and Understanding in Siblings and Peers ... 203

11. NURTURING INDEPENDENCE IN THE ADHD LANDSCAPE ... 211
Life Skills for Independence: An ADHD Perspective ... 212
Teaching Financial Responsibility and Planning ... 216
Self-Care Routines for Teens with ADHD ... 219
Preparing for College and Career: Building a Supportive Transition ... 223

12. **NURTURING THE NURTURER: THE VITALITY OF PARENTAL SELF-CARE IN ADHD PARENTING** — 229
   Building Your Support Network: Finding Your Tribe — 233
   Advocating for Your Child in Healthcare and Education — 237
   Embracing Your Role as an ADHD Advocate: Making a Difference — 241

   Conclusion — 249
   References — 253

INTRODUCTION

Have you ever had one of those mornings where everything falls apart before you even get your first sip of coffee? Honestly, that's the norm around here. The other day, my kitchen was pure chaos—breakfast got burnt, the kids' backpacks were still a mess, and the bus was about to arrive any minute. My middle child was melting because his socks "felt wrong," while my oldest spun on the floor, loudly pretending to be a seal. And right on cue, the baby started crying and tossing his food, demanding to be held. Meanwhile, I was racing around, overwhelmed and desperate for some peace and quiet.

Welcome to parenting in the real world—throw in a child with ADHD, and the chaos ramps up even more. It's unpredictable and exhausting; every day feels like you're just bracing for the next storm. But if you're here reading this, I'm pretty sure you know exactly how it is and what it's like. I want you to know that I'm right there with you, and in the middle of all this craziness, we'll find those moments of laughter, love, and resilience together.

As a mom of three wonderfully unique kids, one of whom has ADHD, I'm intimately familiar with the challenges and joys of parenting in a high-energy, often chaotic environment. Beyond my home, I also balance a career as a scientist and professor. I'm right there with you, in the trenches, trying to apply my research skills to the reality of parenting. My goal with this book is to merge these worlds, offering scientifically-backed strategies and real-life anecdotes to support you, fellow parents on similar paths, and to show you how research can be practically applied to parenting.

This book's heart beats with a clear purpose: to offer you practical tools and empathetic understanding to help manage explosive behavior, foster self-regulation, and above all, celebrate the neurodiversity of our incredible children. I know firsthand the mix of frustration, worry, and immense love that comes with this territory. But you're not alone. Through these pages, I hope to sit with you in those tough moments, share in your victories, and provide a guiding light on the days when everything feels overwhelming. I am in this with you.

In weaving together personal stories, proven strategies, and a sprinkle of scientific insight, I aim to build a bridge between understanding and action. This isn't just a book; it's a support group in a world that might not always understand the brilliance of our children's differences. This book is structured to be your companion, with each chapter designed to empower you and your child to thrive in a world that might not always be understood.

So, here's my call to action for you: dive in with an open heart and a willing spirit. Let's apply these strategies, reflect on the ups and downs, and embrace this beautiful, messy journey of parenting a child with ADHD. Together, we can shift perspectives, celebrate every victory, no matter how small, and foster a world where our children feel seen, supported, and valued for exactly who they are.

Welcome to our shared journey of discovery and growth. Let's celebrate the unique path each of our children is on, armed with love, understanding, and a good dose of humor to keep us sane. Here's to the adventure ahead and the incredible growth we're about to witness—not just in our children, but in ourselves as well. Buckle up, it's going to be a wild ride!

CHAPTER 1

The day you receive an ADHD diagnosis for your child might seem like any other, with the sun neither too shy nor too bold. Yet, within the walls of a doctor's office, your world shifts in ways only a parent can truly understand. You knew in your mama (or Dad) bones, but hearing it aloud is different. It's a deeply personal journey, a recalibration of expectations, dreams, and daily life. This chapter is dedicated to understanding that shift, moving beyond the diagnosis, and diving into what having ADHD means for our children and also what it means to parent a child with ADHD.

UNDERSTANDING ADHD

Attention Deficit Hyperactivity Disorder (ADHD) is often shrouded in a veil of misconceptions and myths, portrayed as a condition of mere distractibility or, worse, a convenient label for challenging behavior. Yet, to stand in the shoes of someone with ADHD is to experience a world where the volume knob on life is turned up just a tad too high, where every stimulus demands attention. Stillness is as elusive as a mirage. ADHD is a neurodevelopmental disorder characterized by patterns of inattention, hyperactivity, and impulsivity that diverge significantly from age-appropriate behavior. The Centers for Disease Control and Prevention (CDC) notes that ADHD is one of the most common neurodevelopmental disorders of childhood. Still, it is essential to recognize its presence and impact into adulthood.

The gradient of ADHD symptoms encompasses a wide range of behaviors and challenges, from forgetfulness and difficulty focusing on tasks to impulsivity and seemingly boundless energy. Yet, within this spectrum lies a diversity of strengths—creativity, empathy, and the capacity for hyperfocus on passionate interests. The strengths and gifts took me a while to learn, and I realized they were there. At the beginning of my family's journey, I wished I had been educated deeper on the strengths and the positives. So, in this book, we'll zoom in on these strengths and, of course, find humor wherever possible because laughter is medicine. By debunking the myth that ADHD lacks focus or discipline, we open the door to a more nuanced understanding and appreciation of the condition.

THE ADHD BRAIN

Recent advances in neuroscience have illuminated how the ADHD brain diverges from typical neurological development. This divergence does not indicate a lesser capability but rather a different wiring. Neuroimaging studies, as highlighted by the National Institute of Mental Health (NIMH), show that the brains of individuals with ADHD may have structural differences and variations in brain activity, especially in areas related to attention, executive function, and impulse control. This neurodiversity underscores the importance of moving beyond a one-size-fits-all approach in education and parenting, advocating for strategies that harness the unique strengths and accommodate the distinct challenges of those with ADHD. It's a reminder to appreciate and respect the unique strengths that individuals with ADHD bring to the table.

The concept of neurodiversity, initially coined by sociologist Judy Singer, suggests that neurological variations such as ADHD, autism, and dyslexia, are not defects but natural variations in the human genome. This perspective fosters an environment of acceptance and adaptation rather than one of correction or cure, encouraging society to value and support all kinds of minds. As I told my non-ADHD six-year-old, you and your older brother's brains are just different from one another and that means you make decisions differently and can see the world differently.

Understanding neurodiversity goes beyond simple awareness—it involves actively challenging the idea that there's only one "right" way to think, learn, or interact. By embracing this perspective, we can create environments at home, in schools, and in our communities that respect these differences and provide everyone the right tools and support. It's important to teach our kids that diversity in thinking is valuable and that those differences can be a source of strength. Whether it's a child's creative approach to problem-solving or unique way of expressing emotions, recognizing these variations as natural and valuable helps build a culture of acceptance and understanding.

DIFFERENT BRAINS

One sunny afternoon, we were in the park, and my older son, Jake, was running around wildly, climbing on everything in sight, and occasionally ignoring the rules we had set for safety. Meanwhile, my younger son, Ethan, was quietly playing with his toy cars on the grass. Suddenly, Jake decided to climb the tallest tree, despite my repeated warnings not to. I had to rush over to him, pulling him down before he got hurt.

After the incident, as Jake sulked on a bench, I noticed Ethan watching everything with a confused expression. I sat down next to Ethan and decided it was a good time to talk to him about what had happened. "Ethan, do you remember how we talk about how everyone's brain works a little differently?" I began. Ethan nodded, his big eyes fixed on me.

"Well, your brain and Jake's brain work in different ways. You see, Jake has ADHD, which means his brain sometimes makes it hard for him to think before he acts or to remember the rules we talk about. It's like his brain is always going super fast, and sometimes it makes decisions without stopping to think if they are good choices."

Ethan furrowed his brow, trying to understand. "But why doesn't my brain do that?" he asked.

"Your brain works differently," I explained. "It's a bit easier for you to stop and think about what you're doing before you do it. You can remember the rules more easily because your brain doesn't move quite as fast as Jake's. That's why sometimes you can make good choices in moments like these, while Jake struggles a bit more."

Ethan looked over at Jake, who was now poking at the ground with a stick. "So, Jake's brain is just different, not bad?"

"Exactly," I said, giving him a hug. "It's not bad at all. It just means he needs a bit more help and patience to make good choices. And you can help him, too, by being understanding and patient with him."

Ethan smiled, seeming to grasp the idea. He got up and walked over to Jake, offering him one of his toy cars. Jake looked up, surprised, then smiled and took the car. They started playing together, their differences momentarily set aside as they enjoyed the simple act of playing side by side.

At that moment, I felt a surge of hope. Explaining these differences to Ethan had helped him understand and accept his brother a little better. It was a small step, but an important one, in fostering empathy and patience between them. And as chaotic as our life could be, it was these moments of connection that made it all worthwhile.

DIAGNOSIS JOURNEY

The path to an ADHD diagnosis often begins with a parent or teacher noticing something distinct about a child's behavior or learning style. It's a path fraught with emotions —worry, confusion, and sometimes relief at finally having a name for the challenges faced. However, obtaining a diagnosis is rarely straightforward. It involves comprehensive evaluations, often including interviews, questionnaires, and behavior rating scales, conducted by professionals such as psychologists, psychiatrists, or pediatricians. To be 100%

frank with you, this process initially brought pushback from me. It was a point of contention for some time between my husband and me and to be clear, I initially struggled with the labeling. This is in part why I wanted to write this book. What I learned and came to understand, though, was that this process is less about labeling; it's really about unlocking a door to tailored support, resources, and understanding; one where a family is handed a new toolbox of sorts. For my family, as we opened this toolbox and learned more about the needs and nuances of ADHD and how it specifically impacts our family, it enormously helped us all.

The moment of diagnosis can be a pivot point for many families. It offers clarity, but it also demands adaptation. Parents find themselves sifting through a deluge of information, advice, and sometimes, misconceptions. It's a journey that underscores the importance of reputable sources and support networks, guiding families through this initial phase of adaptation and understanding.

We found ourselves going through a stack of conflicting emotions. For example, I initially felt some guilt about how I had been handling some of the behaviors we had been dealing with and I felt sad about some of the difficulties I saw my little guy struggling with.

IMPACT ON FAMILY

An ADHD diagnosis does not exist in a vacuum; it ripples through the family, touching every aspect of daily life. Parental stress can escalate, born not out of frustration with the child (although this may also be a thing), but out of a deep-seated desire to protect, support, and advocate for them in a world that might not always understand their needs. Contention might escalate some between parents, as it did in our house, over what this means in how certain behaviors are handled with discipline. Sibling dynamics can shift as well, with brothers and sisters sometimes taking on roles of caretaker, advocate, or, inadvertently, competitor for attention.

Yet, amidst these challenges lies the potential for growth, understanding, and deeper connection. Families often find themselves developing a unique resilience, an ability to communicate and problem-solve that is both nuanced and profound. This transformation is not immediate but evolves, shaped by experiences, successes, and setbacks. It calls for patience, empathy, and an open heart, qualities that, once cultivated, become invaluable assets to any family navigating the complexities of ADHD.

Reflective Exercise: Mapping Your ADHD Journey

Take some time to reflect on your family's journey with ADHD. Grab a notebook or journal and remember when this path began. What were the early signs that made you consider seeking a diagnosis? Write down the key moments from that initial discovery to where you are now. Note the challenges you've faced, the strategies that worked (such as [medication, therapy, support groups]) and even those that didn't (like [ignoring the issue, not seeking professional help]), and those moments of joy and connection that stand out.

As you map this out, consider how each family member has been affected and how they've handled the ups and downs. Have they developed new strengths? How have they grown emotionally, socially, or even creatively? This exercise is more than just a timeline of events—it's a way to acknowledge the resilience, creativity, and love that has carried you through each stage. Reflecting in this way allows you to see the bigger picture, highlighting the progress and growth that can often get overlooked in the daily hustle. This reflection can inspire and motivate you to continue your journey with ADHD.

THE EMOTIONAL JOURNEY OF PARENTING A CHILD WITH ADHD

When you first get an ADHD diagnosis for your child, it can feel overwhelming and bring up a mix of emotions. You might experience denial, fear, and even sadness as you adjust your expectations and rethink what the future might look like. Acceptance doesn't usually come overnight; it's something that develops gradually through reflection, learning, and making small adjustments along the way. It's not just about accepting a label—it's about learning how to better connect with your child and understanding how they see and experience the world.

As you move forward, this process becomes a journey of growth for both you and your child. You'll start to notice the unique strengths and perspectives they bring, even if they don't always align with traditional expectations. It's important to give yourself grace as you navigate this new understanding, allowing room for both challenges and progress.

With time, you'll build a deeper connection based on a more authentic understanding of your child's needs and abilities. This shift is what helps create a home environment where everyone feels supported and valued for who they truly are.

In the heart of this emotional medley lies the crucial role of empathy. Cultivating genuine compassion for your child's experiences means more than putting yourself in their shoes; it's an endeavor to deeply understand their world where filters are scarce, and stimuli are overwhelming. It's about pushing away the notion that behavior is simply a child misbehaving, which real-talk was and is complicated for me sometimes, and in reality, is a symptom of a more significant issue they can't control, like how their very brain is put together. It's about acknowledging the Herculean effort required for them to navigate a day filled with expectations and norms that clash with their innate wiring. This empathy becomes a bridge, enhancing the connection between you and your child and serving as a beacon guiding you through the tumultuous moments. It is the lens through which challenges transform into opportunities for growth and bonding, where every obstacle surmounted together reinforces the foundation of your relationship.

Amid these adjustments, parental stress burgeons, not from a lack of love or patience, but from an abundance of concern, a relentless quest for strategies that might soothe, support, or stimulate in just the right measure. And let me be clear here, you may have a lack of patience at times. Heck, we are parents and human-beings. This is part of the job, but bringing in empathy and a lens of how they might be experiencing the world helps to soften the angst and bring increased understanding. Managing this stress demands intentional efforts; it is an art form that balances acceptance with action. Techniques such as mindfulness, practiced in stolen moments of calm, or physical activities, which serve both as an outlet for tension and a non-verbal bond with your child, become invaluable. Equally important is the nurturing of interests and hobbies that are solely yours; these are not acts of escapism but essential exercises in self-preservation and renewal.

When we first learned our son had extreme ADHD at the tender age of three, I remember feeling a mix of concern and confusion—especially when our therapist suggested we focus on strengthening our marriage. There we were, ready to dive into whatever therapies and strategies we could to support our little guy, and the advice was... work on our marriage. At first, it felt misplaced, maybe even a bit frustrating. But as she explained, the strain on couples can be intense, and often, these precious kids feel responsible if things go south at home. That hit hard. It made me realize just how interconnected our family's well-being truly is. So, while it might sound a bit backward at first, prioritizing self-care isn't just about keeping your cup full—it's like the airplane rule of putting on your oxygen mask first before helping others. It's a crucial act of self-preservation that benefits everyone in the family. So, remember: putting your well-being at the forefront isn't selfish; it's necessary for the greater good of your whole crew.

Navigating the world of ADHD parenting is tough, and it's not something most people do alone. Finding support—both practical and emotional—is crucial. After a diagnosis, it's easy to feel like pulling back, either because of stigma, guilt, or a mix of both. But connecting with others who get it can make a big difference. Whether through support groups, online communities, or talking with friends and family, these connections offer more than a space to vent. They provide fundamental strategies, helpful resources, and, sometimes, just the comfort of knowing you're not alone.

Beyond peer support, professionals like therapists, counselors, and ADHD coaches can guide you through the ups and downs. They offer expert advice on managing everything from daily routines to the emotional rollercoaster that can come with ADHD. Their guidance turns overwhelming into something manageable, helping you break down challenges into smaller, achievable steps. Reaching out for this kind of help doesn't just lighten the load—it equips you with the tools to confidently support your child and build a stronger foundation for your family.

Sometimes your closest friends, the ones who had kids around the same time as you, just can't grasp what you're going through. Their child might sleep through the night, sit calmly at the table, and make social gatherings seem easy and enjoyable. Meanwhile, you're feeling frazzled, isolated, and maybe even questioning if you're doing something wrong. If this hits home for you, please know that you're not alone. There are others out there who understand the unique challenges you're facing. Your people are out there—you just need to find the communities and support systems that get it.

Over time, you might even notice that your closest friends start to learn from you. As they see what you're navigating, they'll begin to understand your world a bit more. They might ask questions, offer more empathy, and adjust how they show up for you. The gap in understanding won't always feel so wide, and as your friends learn from your experiences, you'll feel less isolated. Your journey can even be a source of insight for those who care about you, deepening those friendships in ways you might not have expected.

This mosaic of emotions, connections, and support that parents build in the wake of an ADHD diagnosis is intricate and multifaceted. It reflects a spectrum of experiences that, while unique to each family, share common threads of resilience, empathy, and an unyielding commitment to understanding and supporting their child's journey through life with ADHD.

ADHD AND FAMILY DYNAMICS: NAVIGATING SIBLING RELATIONSHIPS

In a family, each member brings their own unique personality, strengths, and needs. When a child is diagnosed with ADHD, the family's focus can naturally shift to meet the more immediate and sometimes intense demands that come with it. This can sometimes create an imbalance where one child's needs take center stage. However, effective parenting in this situation means supporting every family member while recognizing the different ways they each need attention and care.

Balancing this isn't about giving everyone equal time or attention but ensuring that each child's needs are met in ways that matter most to them. For the child with ADHD, this might involve extra patience, specialized strategies, or consistent routines. For siblings, it could mean setting aside one-on-one time where they have your full attention, engaging in activities they love, or simply being there to listen to what's on their mind. The goal is to ensure that every child feels valued and connected, regardless of how different their needs might be. Creating these moments of meaningful connection, you help each child feel understood, supported, and meaningful within the family.

Educating siblings about ADHD unfolds as a delicate process, one that invites understanding without casting the child with ADHD as either a burden or a project. This education takes root not in clinical terms but in the language of empathy and shared experiences. It's about framing ADHD in a way that siblings can relate to, perhaps comparing the challenges of focusing on a task when the brain feels like a browser with too many tabs open, or understanding impulsivity as the feeling of words slipping out before they can be caught. This approach fosters an empathetic understanding, cultivating a family culture where differences are not just acknowledged but appreciated.

In our family, our oldest—who has ADHD—is the one leading the charge with endless energy, day in and day out. Right behind him is our five-year-old, who's quickly picking up on his brother's more "spirited" behaviors. It's definitely a challenge! Recently, I sat them down for a talk about how their brains work differently. The goal wasn't to compare or point out flaws but to highlight the strengths each of them brings. I explained that while my middle child's brain might process things differently, that doesn't mean he has to copy every impulsive reaction he sees. It's important to understand these differences and be empathetic towards them. He seemed to understand that having a slightly slower processing speed gives him an edge—it helps him stop and think before acting.

During one of their usual debates about fairness, I took a moment to point out what they are really good at, hoping to build them up. Celebrating their strengths is not just a strategy, it's a powerful tool that can inspire and motivate them. Did it work? Who knows, but I could see my middle guy pause and maybe rethink whether he wanted to follow the same explosive path. I'm keeping my fingers crossed that these little moments of reflection stick and lead to something positive!

Conflict, while a natural part of any relationship, takes on unique dimensions in families touched by ADHD. The sources are multifaceted—stemming from misunderstandings, jealousy, or simply the exhaustion that permeates high-energy households. And the exhaustion is real.

Tools for resolving these conflicts lean heavily on communication, but not the hurried exchanges that often fill the day. Instead, it calls for intentional dialogues, spaces where each child can voice grievances without fear of dismissal or reproach. Such conversations are guided by active listening, where the goal is not to respond but to understand, and to see the world through the sibling's eyes. This understanding becomes the foundation for solutions that acknowledge each child's feelings and needs, crafting compromises that are lived, not just agreed upon.

Creating unity within the family, amidst the diverse challenges and dynamics that ADHD introduces, is an ongoing endeavor. It's woven through the small, daily rituals that become the heartbeat of the family—meals shared without the distraction of screens, evening walks that invite casual conversation, or weekend projects that see each member contributing in their own way. Unity is also fostered in celebrations that mark not just achievements but efforts, recognizing the unique contributions of each child. Whether it's the perseverance of the child with ADHD in completing a task, the patience of a sibling in helping out, or the creative flair another brings to a family project, each is celebrated. These celebrations are not grand gestures but quiet acknowledgments, notes of appreciation left on pillows, or the warmth of a hug that says, "I see you, I value you, and I'm proud of you."

In this intricate dance of balancing attention, educating siblings, managing conflicts, and creating unity, the rhythm is set by understanding, empathy, and communication. It's a fluid motion, adapting to the changing needs and dynamics of the family, always with the aim of weaving a stronger, more cohesive family unit. Here, each child, with their unique needs, challenges, and strengths, finds their place, contributing their unique thread to the family tapestry, vibrant and whole.

BUILDING A SUPPORTIVE HOME ENVIRONMENT FOR NEURODIVERSITY

The heart of a family's connection often comes from the shared spaces where everyone feels safe and supported. In a home where ADHD is part of the mix, creating these spaces takes on extra importance. It's about intentionally setting up environments that not only work for a child with ADHD but also highlight their strengths. This means designing calming and engaging areas tailored to their sensory needs and attention levels. Whether it's a cozy reading nook, a clutter-free play area, or a quiet corner for downtime, these spaces are meant to help your child feel comfortable, understood, and at ease, boosting their self-esteem in the process.

Practically, this might look like organizing a study space with minimal distractions, using soft lighting, or incorporating tools like fidget items or noise-canceling headphones. It's also about having clear routines and visual cues to help your child stay focused and secure. Start with one change at a time, allowing your child to adjust before introducing the next. The goal is to create an environment where everyone in the family can thrive while honoring the unique way your child experiences the world. This approach doesn't just meet your child's needs—it turns your home into a place where everyone feels valued and connected.

When my oldest was around four, we set up a sensory swing in our kitchen—a simple nylon cocoon swing that became a lifesaver. Whenever things got chaotic or needed to reset, we'd pop it up, and the kids would take turns swinging quietly while flipping through books. It was a calming space that gave everyone a moment to regroup. Sensory spaces like this are great for all kids, not just those with ADHD. Every child needs to learn how to self-soothe and regulate emotions, regardless of their challenges.

When my oldest started kindergarten, we realized how helpful that morning swing time was for him. A few minutes in the swing before heading to school made a noticeable difference in how he managed his day. It allowed him to calm his body and get into the right headspace, setting him up for a smoother transition into the structured school environment. Creating small sensory routines like this can be a powerful tool for managing behavior and helping all kids feel more grounded and ready to take on the day.

The cornerstone of this endeavor rests in the thoughtful creation of inclusive spaces. These are areas within the home intentionally arranged to mitigate sensory overload while promoting concentration and calm. Consider the tactile, auditory, and visual stimuli that pervade each room. Soft lighting replaces harsh fluorescents to soothe sensitive eyes, while designated quiet zones offer respite from the auditory bombardment of daily life. Furniture and toys are selected with a preference for textures that comfort rather than irritate, creating tactile environments that invite touch and exploration without overwhelming. Walls might be adorned with artworks or colors chosen not for their trendiness but for their ability to calm or invigorate, specifically tailored to the emotional and sensory needs of the child. In these spaces, every element is a note in the symphony of a supportive home, composed with the intent of nurturing the child's well-being and focus.

Yet, the physical aspect of space is but one dimension. Equally vital is the rhythm that pulses through these environments—the delicate cadence of routine and flexibility. Stability, often found in the predictability of routine, offers an anchor in the turbulent seas of ADHD, reducing anxiety and providing a framework that guides the child through the day. Mornings might follow a scripted dance, with visual schedules depicting each step, from brushing teeth to packing school bags, transforming the often chaotic start into a smooth running stream of preparation. However, rigidity fractures under the weight of ADHD's inherent unpredictability, necessitating an infusion of flexibility. It is understanding that some days, breakfast might be on the go, or homework might pause for a needed break, without the guilt that deviation from routine often carries. This balance does not come predefined; it evolves, shaped by the family's experiences, learning where the structure can support and where flexibility needs to breathe. It is a dance of sorts.

Central to this evolution is the adoption of a strength-based approach. This perspective shifts the focus from the deficits and challenges of ADHD to the strengths and interests that each child brings. It's about celebrating the child's imaginative storytelling, their intricate drawings, or their ability to solve complex puzzles, integrating these strengths into daily routines and the physical environment. Shelves might be filled with books that feed their curiosity, while walls become galleries showcasing their creativity. In these actions, the message is clear: you are valued, your interests matter, and your strengths can light the way. This approach does not ignore the challenges but embeds solutions within the celebration of strengths, fostering a sense of self-worth and independence in the child.

Maintaining open communication is just as crucial alongside the physical setup and routines. It's not just about what's said but about creating a space where listening takes center stage. Kids need to feel safe sharing their emotions and struggles without fear of judgment. This means allowing space for everything—a meltdown or a small win—so that they know their feelings are valid and heard. Family dinners, for example, can become a time when everyone talks openly about the ups and downs of their day, where both frustrations and victories are given the same attention and respect. This simple routine can be a powerful tool in fostering open communication.

This kind of open dialogue isn't limited to just within the family. It's also about looping in teachers, friends, and others who are part of your child's world, helping them understand your child's needs and supporting them in a way that makes sense. These conversations are not just about the present, but also about building a foundation for your child's future. They teach kids how to recognize and express their own emotions while also learning how to empathize with others. Over time, these ongoing exchanges build their emotional intelligence, giving them tools to navigate the social challenges of ADHD and helping them feel more confident in their interactions, both at home and beyond.

In constructing a home environment that supports neurodiversity, the journey is both personal and collective. It requires patience, creativity, and an unyielding commitment to seeing the world through the child's eyes. Each adaptation, each conversation, each moment of understanding, builds upon the last, crafting a living environment that grows and evolves with the family. This home becomes more than a physical space; it is a testament to the family's journey, a space where every member, neurodiverse or not, finds their needs met, their strengths celebrated, and their voice heard. In this environment, the child with ADHD thrives, supported not just by walls and routines, but by the unwavering love and understanding that permeates every aspect of their home.

CHAPTER 2
THE ALCHEMY OF COMMUNICATION: TRANSFORMING UNDERSTANDING INTO ACTION

Recently, while listening to a band rehearsal in my mom's basement, I couldn't help but think about how much it mirrors family life. Every family member has their own rhythm, and when parents—especially those managing the high-energy dynamics of ADHD—set the right tone, all that noise can come together into something that works. But when the vibe is off and everyone's out of sync, it can feel like pure chaos.

This chapter is your practical guide to fine-tuning communication in your family. It's all about mastering the back-and-forth that helps build real understanding and stronger connections. It's in those everyday conversations, gestures, and even the quiet moments where empathy comes into play, making sure every kid feels seen, heard, and genuinely understood.

MASTERING EMPATHETIC LISTENING TO UNDERSTAND YOUR CHILD

Active Listening Skills

Listening, truly listening, is an art form that goes beyond simply hearing words. It involves engaging with the heart, tuning into the emotions and unspoken messages behind the words. For a child with ADHD, whose thoughts may dart like fireflies, being heard can feel like a lifeline—a confirmation that their feelings and experiences matter. Active listening is the anchor in these conversations, requiring parents to be fully present, and setting aside distractions to focus entirely on the child - not always an easy task. It's about making eye contact, nodding, and providing small verbal affirmations like "I see" or "Tell me more." This approach doesn't just validate the child's feelings; it opens a window into their world, offering insights into their thoughts, fears, and dreams.

Oh, the adventures of conversation in our house! Our ADHD superhero has this thing—he'll launch into a chat with all the subtlety of a fireworks display, loud and over anyone else already talking. It used to frazzle me, especially during those calm moments that suddenly weren't so calm. But then, one day, he blurts out mid-interruption, "I have to say it NOW, because I'll forget." And just like that, it clicked. He wasn't trying to steamroll the conversation or be impolite; he was genuinely worried that his thoughts would slip away before he got a chance to share them, like trying to catch a leaf in a gust of wind.

This was our lightbulb moment about active listening. It's more than just hearing words; it's about understanding the urgency and the struggle behind them. Now, we make a conscious effort to give him space to express himself before his thoughts dart off to the next big idea. It's not about allowing chaos at the dinner table, but about acknowledging his need to be heard and included, ensuring he doesn't feel left out or forgotten in the swirl of daily family life.

Building on that, we've woven a little ritual into our daily routine to keep everyone feeling connected and heard. Every day after school, we all take turns sharing the highs and lows of our day. Everyone gets their moment in the spotlight, a chance to talk about that one good thing that made them smile, and maybe a not-so-good thing that didn't. It's simple, but it's our way of making sure no one feels like they're just part of the background.

This practice has turned into more than just sharing updates; it's a way for us to actively listen to each other in a structured setting, which really helps our son with ADHD focus and participate without fear of forgetting his thoughts and for his younger brother to not feel steamrolled and also get to share on his own. I like to think of it as a knit blanket that is our family, and over time we're weaving a stronger family fabric with each day's stories—ensuring everyone's voice is heard and valued, piece by piece.

One practical strategy involves setting aside a specific time each day for open-ended conversations. This could be during a walk, at bedtime, or over a meal. For us, sometimes it is the walk back from the bus stop or the drive to get the baby. The setting matters less than the intentionality behind the gesture, signaling to the child that their thoughts and feelings are worthy of attention and time.

Reflective Responses

Reflective responses are the mirror in which a child's feelings and statements are reflected back, validating their experiences while encouraging deeper exploration. This technique involves paraphrasing or summarizing what the child has said, not to interrogate but to clarify and deepen understanding. For instance, if a child expresses frustration over a failed task, a reflective response might be, "It sounds like you're really upset because that didn't go the way you hoped." This not only shows that the parent is listening but also helps the child process their emotions, fostering a sense of empathy and connection.

Reflective listening has been a game-changer in our communication toolbox, especially for our child with ADHD. Let me paint you a picture: Imagine he's had a rough day, and emotions are running high. He's trying to express what's bothering him, but the words tumble out in a rush. Instead of just nodding along, I mirror back what he's saying, "It sounds like you're really upset because you didn't get to finish your art project today." This simple act of reflecting not only helps him feel heard, but it also gives him a moment to process his emotions and thoughts. It's like holding up a mirror to his feelings, making them clearer to both of us. More importantly, it reassures him that it's okay to feel the way he does and that he's not alone in navigating those big emotions. This technique helps slow down the conversation, making it more manageable for him to engage without losing his train of thought or feeling overwhelmed.

Non-Verbal Communication

Words carry weight, but the unspoken messages conveyed through body language and facial expressions often speak volumes. For children with ADHD, who may struggle with verbal communication, these non-verbal cues become a critical aspect of understanding and connection. A warm smile, a gentle touch, or a nod can communicate support and understanding more eloquently than words. Conversely, a furrowed brow or crossed arms might convey disapproval or disinterest, even if unintentionally. Parents can consciously use their body language to show openness and acceptance, sitting at eye level with the child and maintaining an open posture to encourage communication. I know in our house, a squeeze of the shoulder or the ruffling of the hair can go a long way.

Picture this: It's a typical Saturday morning, and your house is buzzing with the energy of a small, caffeine-fueled carnival. Your ADHD superstar is darting from the kitchen to the living room like a ping-pong ball on a mission. You're in the middle of making breakfast when you realize you've run out of eggs. You catch your kid's eye, point to the empty egg carton, and make an exaggerated sad face. Without a word, they know exactly what you mean and start helping you look for alternatives. Non-verbal communication can be a lifesaver, especially when words seem to bounce off like rubber balls. Whether it's a thumbs-up to show you're proud or a silly dance to defuse a tense moment, these silent signals can bridge the gap when verbal communication hits a snag. Plus, let's face it, sometimes it's just more fun to communicate with a wink and a nod than with a lecture!

Avoiding Communication Breakdowns

Misunderstandings and frustrations are inevitable in any family, yet in the context of ADHD, where impulsivity and emotional dysregulation can escalate conflicts, navigating these moments with care is crucial. Strategies to prevent communication breakdowns include pausing before responding to emotionally charged statements and allowing both parent and child time to process their feelings. It's also helpful to establish a 'cool down' signal—a pre-agreed gesture or word that either party can use when they need a moment to gather their thoughts or emotions. This signal acts as a circuit breaker, preventing heated moments from escalating into full-blown conflicts.

In moments of misunderstanding, it can be beneficial to revisit the conversation later, approaching the topic with fresh perspective and calm. This not only models healthy conflict resolution but also teaches the child that disagreements can be navigated with patience and empathy.

Strategy Section: Active Listening Checklist

To reinforce the concepts of empathetic listening within real-life contexts, a checklist can serve as a tangible reminder to engage in active listening practices. You could use the following list to tailor for yourself or use all of these on your own checklist to remind yourself. Feel free to tailor your own list and hang in a place where it will remind you to foster connection with your child(ren). This tool could include prompts such as:

☐ Made eye contact and put aside distractions

☐ Nod and provided verbal affirmations to show engagement

☐ Use reflective responses to validate feelings and encourage further sharing

☐ Pay attention to my body language, ensuring it conveys openness and understanding

☐ Use our 'cool down' signal when needed, to prevent escalation

☐ Revisit conversations with a calm and fresh perspective when misunderstandings occurred

Incorporating this checklist into daily interactions can help you internalize these practices, making empathetic communication a natural and integral part of your relationship with your child.

Through the mastery of empathetic listening, you can cultivate a home environment where your child feels unequivocally understood and valued. This chapter, like a compass, guides you in navigating the intricate dance of communication, ensuring that each step, each gesture, and each word, contributes to a deeper connection and understanding. Here, in the alchemy of communication, the true magic of empathy unfolds, transforming understanding into tangible, transformative action.

DIALOGUE TOOLS THAT REDUCE CONFLICT AND BUILD TRUST

In family life, significantly when you're raising a child with ADHD, conflicts are bound to happen. These moments can strain relationships or, when approached thoughtfully, bring you closer together. It's not about avoiding disagreements but learning how to handle them in ways that strengthen trust and connection. In this section, we'll dive into practical tools for turning conflicts into opportunities for growth. Instead of seeing these tools as ways to "win" arguments, think of them as ways to create more understanding and respect within your family. Handling challenging moments with care can build resilience and more robust relationships even when things get difficult.

In the realm of conflict resolution, techniques that prioritize empathic understanding over authoritative decrees pave the way for resolutions that not only address the immediate discord but sew the seeds of long-term trust and cooperation. Picture a scenario where tempers flare and voices rise—a common scenario in any household. The instinct might lean toward asserting control to quell the turmoil. Yet, experience whispers a more effective strategy: stepping into the chaos with a calm that belies the storm, inviting dialogue that seeks to uncover not just the what of the conflict but the why. This method involves acknowledging emotions without judgment, validating the feelings that bubble beneath the surface, and engaging in a collaborative search for solutions that honor the needs of all involved. It's a delicate balance, requiring patience and practice, where the goal is not to win but to understand, not to dominate but to share power, crafting solutions that resonate with fairness and empathy.

Boundaries, the invisible lines that define the where, when, and how of behavior, are as vital to the health of a family as the beams that support a house. Yet, when setting these boundaries, especially with a child for whom impulse and inattention blur lines, the approach must be infused with love and respect. Clear boundaries, communicated with transparency and kindness, become signposts rather than barriers, guiding the child through the complexities of acceptable behavior while respecting their need for autonomy and exploration. It is in the how of this communication that love manifests—through words that explain the reasons behind the boundaries, through consistency that builds reliability, and through flexibility that acknowledges the child's growth and changing needs. Here, boundaries become not just tools of discipline but expressions of care, teaching the child not only the limits of their world but the depth of their value within it.

Trust is at the core of every strong family, and it grows through shared experiences, especially when we show up for each other. Building trust often means stepping out of the usual routine and doing activities that require teamwork and support. Think of games or challenges that make you work together—like solving a puzzle as a team or tackling an obstacle course—where the goal isn't about who's best but how well you can communicate, listen, and adapt as a group. These experiences, whether they succeed or not, help solidify the sense that you can handle challenges better when you face them together. And remember, these activities are not just about building trust, they're also about having fun and creating joyful memories.

However, trust isn't only built through activities but also in quiet moments. It's in those one-on-one talks where your child feels safe to open up about their fears or dreams and where you take the time to listen and share your thoughts. These moments are not just conversations, they are opportunities to strengthen the bond and trust within your family. Over time, these connections create a deeper understanding and respect for each other's perspectives. By recognizing and valuing what makes each person unique, trust naturally strengthens and becomes a steady foundation for your family.

There was this one time when our son had a meltdown that could have registered on the Richter scale. He was a whirlwind of anger and frustration, throwing toys and yelling at the top of his lungs. Every attempt to calm him down seemed to add fuel to the fire, so I decided to change tactics. I walked into his room, sat down quietly on the floor, and waited. Minutes felt like hours, but slowly, the storm began to pass. He went from stomping, tearing apart his room, and shouting to a puddle of tears, eventually curling up in my lap, exhausted and emotional. In that tender moment, we talked about the big emotions he was struggling to handle. I held him close and reassured him that it was okay to feel overwhelmed. Together, we started to unpack his feelings, and I let him know that no matter how big his emotions got, his Dad and I would always be there to help him through them. It was a breakthrough, a moment where he learned that his feelings were valid and that he wasn't alone in navigating them.

Positive reinforcement is one of the most effective ways to guide behavior, significantly when raising a child with ADHD. Instead of focusing on what went wrong, it shifts the spotlight to what's going right, even if the progress seems small. In a world where kids with ADHD often face criticism or constant correction, positive reinforcement becomes a way to build their self-esteem and keep them motivated. It's not about pushing or pressuring them but genuinely celebrating their efforts.

A simple word of encouragement, a small note recognizing their hard work, or even a high-five can make a huge difference. When you consistently acknowledge their progress, it sends a clear message: "Your efforts matter, and we see your growth." This approach helps shift their mindset from feeling limited to realizing their potential. Over time, they become more willing to communicate openly, set goals, and trust your support. Positive reinforcement doesn't just change behavior—it builds confidence and a belief that they can keep moving forward, no matter how tough the journey gets.

In deploying these tools of dialogue—conflict resolution techniques that seek understanding, boundaries set with love, trust-building activities, and the judicious use of positive reinforcement—parents sculpt an environment where communication thrives not as a series of commands and responses but as a vibrant exchange of ideas, emotions, and dreams. This environment, rich in trust and mutual respect, becomes the soil in which the seeds of confidence and connection flourish, where every family member, unique in their melody, contributes to the symphony of shared life, harmonious in its diversity and stronger for its challenges.

ENCOURAGING YOUR CHILD TO EXPRESS EMOTIONS CONSTRUCTIVELY

Parenting a child with ADHD comes with unique challenges, especially when it comes to helping them manage their emotions. This process goes beyond just teaching them to identify what they're feeling. It's about guiding them to express those emotions in a way that leads to better communication and stronger connections rather than outbursts or misunderstandings. Remember, the long-term benefits of this process are worth the effort.

To do this effectively, it's essential to start by helping your child recognize and label their feelings—whether it's frustration, excitement, or anxiety. From there, you can work on giving them tools to express those emotions healthily, like using words instead of actions, taking calming breaths, or stepping away when they feel overwhelmed. As a parent, you play a crucial role in modeling and practicing empathy. This involves actively listening to your child, acknowledging their feelings, and showing them how understanding others' emotions can make communication smoother and reduce tension.

By consistently practicing these skills, your child learns how to handle their emotions more constructively, making it easier to build positive relationships and feel more in control of their interactions. While it takes time and patience, the payoff is worth it as they develop better self-regulation and emotional awareness.

Emotional Regulation Tools

The endeavor to equip children with ADHD with the tools for emotional regulation begins with the foundational skill of identification. Recognizing emotions as they arise, and naming them with precision, is the first step toward gaining control over them. This skill can be cultivated through activities as simple as sharing stories or watching films together, pausing to discuss the characters' emotions, and relating them to real-life experiences. Such discussions provide a dual benefit: they not only enhance the child's emotional vocabulary but also offer a safe distance from which to explore complex feelings. Further, integrating emotion cards or charts into daily routines can serve as a visual aid, helping the child to match their internal experiences with tangible expressions. This process, akin to decoding a mysterious language, empowers the child, offering them a sense of mastery over their emotional world.

The transition from identification to expression is facilitated by teaching children various outlets for their feelings. Art, music, and movement serve as powerful mediums through which emotions can be explored and expressed safely. A child might draw to represent their anger or play an instrument to communicate sadness, translating intangible feelings into concrete creations. Such activities not only validate the child's emotions but also teach them that feelings, no matter how intense, can be managed and communicated in positive, creative ways.

Modeling Emotional Expression

As in all aspects of child development, the role of the parent as a model is indispensable. Demonstrating healthy emotional expression and coping mechanisms in one's own life teaches more effectively than any lesson or lecture. When a parent articulates their feelings during challenging moments—"I'm feeling frustrated right now because things aren't going as planned, but I'm going to take a deep breath and think of a solution"—they provide a live demonstration of emotional regulation in action. This modeling extends to showing vulnerability, allowing children to see that seeking help or expressing when one is overwhelmed is not a sign of weakness but an aspect of strength and self-awareness. Through these lived examples, children learn that emotions are not to be feared or suppressed but understood and managed with grace.

If you're reading this and feeling like you haven't quite nailed this yet, don't stress. We're all human, and we all mess up—myself included. What's important to remember is that it's never too late to start fresh. In fact, it's valuable for our kids to see us stumble and then work on making things right. Dr. Becky Kennedy discusses this in *Good Inside*, emphasizing the power of repair. Whether apologizing, reconnecting with our child, or patching things up with our spouse or someone else, our kids are learning how we handle those moments. When they see us come back, acknowledge our mistakes, and make a genuine effort to repair, they know that relationships can recover and even grow stronger after challenging moments.

Each day gives us a chance to rewire our children's and our own brains, no matter what's happened in the past. With small, consistent changes, we can start responding differently, building more trust and connection over time. So, take a deep breath and be kind to yourself. Every attempt to repair and reconnect is a step in the right direction. It's okay to start from where you are, focusing on creating a more positive and supportive environment for your child and yourself.

Safe Spaces for Emotion

The creation of physical and emotional sanctuaries where children can experience and express their feelings without fear of judgment or reprimand is crucial. Physical spaces might be as simple as a cozy corner with pillows and comfort items where a child can retreat when feeling overwhelmed. Emotionally, a safe space is woven from threads of unconditional support, understanding, and reassurance. It's in these spaces that children are encouraged to voice their feelings, knowing they will be met with empathy and support. Family meetings can serve as regular forums for sharing feelings and concerns, reinforcing the idea that every emotion is valid and worthy of attention. In these sanctuaries, emotions are not enemies to be battled but messengers to be heard, offering insights into the child's inner world.

Building Emotional Intelligence

The culmination of these efforts is the development of emotional intelligence—the ability to understand and manage one's emotions and empathize with those of others. This skill is fostered not only through direct teaching and modeling but also through interactive games and activities that encourage perspective-taking and empathy. Role-playing scenarios, for example, can help children consider different viewpoints, fostering an understanding of how their actions and emotions affect others. Additionally, incorporating discussions about emotions into daily conversations reinforces the importance of emotional awareness and regulation. Over time, these practices contribute to an enhanced self-awareness in the child, an understanding of the complexity of emotions, and a toolkit of strategies for navigating them constructively.

In guiding a child with ADHD through the complexities of their emotional landscape, the aim is to illuminate the path toward constructive expression and self-regulation. Through a combination of teaching, modeling, creating safe spaces, and fostering emotional intelligence, parents can support their children in developing a deep understanding of their emotions, transforming potential obstacles into opportunities for growth and connection. This journey, marked by patience and empathy, not only equips the child to navigate their inner world but also enhances their relationships with those around them, laying a foundation for a life rich in emotional depth and understanding.

Making these skills even more important, research and literature reveal that children with ADHD often lag behind their peers by about 30% in terms of executive functioning skills. This means that an eight-year-old child with ADHD might exhibit the emotional and organizational skills typical of a five or six-year-old. This developmental lag underscores the importance of teaching and reinforcing emotional intelligence and self-regulation skills. For these children, mastering these skills is not just beneficial but essential. By focusing on building emotional intelligence, parents and educators can help bridge this gap, providing the necessary tools for these children to better manage their emotions and behaviors. This foundation of emotional understanding and regulation is crucial for their overall development and success, both academically and socially.

NAVIGATING SCHOOL MEETINGS: ADVOCACY AND COLLABORATION

In the realm of education, particularly for parents of children with ADHD, the orchestration of Individualized Education Programs (IEP) or 504 Plan meetings transforms into an intricate ballet of preparation, communication, and advocacy. The dance floor, often populated by educators, administrators, and specialists, requires not just presence but active engagement from parents, who step into these spaces armed with the dual mantles of advocate and collaborator.

Preparing for IEP/504 Meetings

Preparation for these pivotal meetings begins not at the school's gates but within the quiet sanctum of home, where parents gather the montage of their child's educational, medical, and developmental records. This preparatory phase involves a meticulous collection of documents—report cards, teacher notes, assessments by healthcare providers, and personal observations of the child's learning patterns. The aggregation of these records serves a dual purpose; it not only equips parents with the evidence needed to advocate for their child's requirements but also paints a holistic picture of the child's needs, strengths, and challenges. Additionally, drafting a list of key questions and concerns before the meeting ensures that no critical topic is left unaddressed, from the specifics of curriculum modifications to the provision of assistive technologies or support services.

Effective Communication with Teachers

The cornerstone of effective advocacy lies in the cultivation of a partnership with teachers and school staff, a relationship characterized by mutual respect, open dialogue, and a shared commitment to the child's growth. This alliance is nurtured through regular, proactive communication, extending beyond the confines of formal meetings to include informal check-ins and updates. The intention here is not to oversee but to collaborate, offering insights into the child's experiences at home that might inform strategies in the classroom. In these exchanges, the emphasis shifts from presenting demands to engaging in a dialogue that explores possibilities, adaptations, and interventions that cater to the child's unique needs. Parents, by sharing anecdotes of the child's interests, successes, and challenges outside school, provide teachers with a broader understanding of the child, facilitating more personalized and effective teaching approaches.

From my own experience, building strong relationships with my son's teachers has been an absolute Godsend. Early on, I made it a point to introduce myself and open lines of communication with his teachers, emphasizing that I was there to support them as much as my son. These connections grew into genuine partnerships, with regular emails and chats about my son's progress and any emerging concerns. One of his teachers even took the time to meet with us outside of school hours to better understand his unique needs and strengths. This collaborative spirit has led to tailored strategies that truly resonate with my son, making his school experience more positive and productive. Knowing that his teachers are allies who genuinely care about his well-being has been incredibly reassuring and has made a world of difference in both his academic journey and on my mama heart.

Advocacy Strategies

Advocacy, at its core, is the art of speaking up, a delicate balance of assertiveness and diplomacy. For parents, it involves not just voicing the needs and rights of their child but doing so in a manner that invites cooperation rather than confrontation. This approach is characterized by a well-informed stance, grounded in an understanding of the child's legal rights to education and accommodation under laws such as the Individuals with Disabilities Education Act

(IDEA) and Section 504 of the Rehabilitation Act. Armed with this knowledge, parents can navigate discussions with confidence, proposing accommodations and modifications grounded in legal precedent and educational best practices. Moreover, effective advocacy is underscored by the principle of specificity—articulating not just what is needed but why it is needed, linking each request to an aspect of the child's learning experience or educational goals.

Fostering School-Home Partnerships

The bridge between home and school, built on the pillars of trust, respect, and shared goals, serves as the conduit through which the child's educational journey is enriched. This partnership thrives on the active involvement of parents in the school community, from participation in classroom activities to involvement in parent-teacher associations. It also benefits from the establishment of consistent communication channels, whether through digital platforms, regular meetings, or home-school diaries, that facilitate the seamless exchange of information regarding the child's progress, challenges, and milestones. Within this framework, the role of parents transcends the traditional boundaries of advocacy, evolving into a collaborative force that champions not just the needs of their own child but contributes to the creation of an inclusive, accommodating educational environment for all students.

Navigating school meetings and advocating for your child's needs can feel overwhelming. However, as a parent, you have much power to shape their academic experience. Being well-prepared, clear in your communication, and strategic in advocating is key. This preparation will give you the confidence and control to ensure your child gets the accommodations and support they need to succeed. Building strong partnerships with teachers and school staff is vital. This process might have its challenges, but it also offers opportunities for growth and empowerment—not just for your child with ADHD but for everyone involved in supporting them. Through these efforts, you're helping your child thrive and contributing to a more inclusive and supportive learning environment for all kids.

Reflecting on this chapter, it's clear that the critical role of parents extends beyond the home. Advocating for and collaborating with educational institutions to support our child's unique learning needs is essential. Preparation, partnership, and informed advocacy are key to navigating the educational landscape, ensuring that every child has access to the resources and accommodations necessary to flourish. As we transition from the school environment to the broader context of social skills and relationship building, the principles of empathy, communication, and collaboration continue to serve as guiding lights, shaping the journey ahead.

CHAPTER 3
CRAFTING CALM IN THE CHAOS

Imagine a river, its currents swift and unpredictable, winding through landscapes both serene and stormy. Now picture a child with ADHD as a navigator on this river, their vessel subject to the whims of an ever-changing flow. The river's unpredictability mirrors the daily life of a child with ADHD, where calm waters can swiftly become turbulent. Here, the creation of routines and structures acts as buoys and lighthouses, guiding the child through the waters, and providing both direction and comfort amid the chaos.

THE IMPORTANCE OF ROUTINE FOR CHILDREN WITH ADHD

Benefits of Routine

Routines, in their essence, are the architecture of daily life, offering a framework upon which the day's activities are built. For children with ADHD, this structure is akin to a map in the hands of a navigator, delineating the path ahead with clarity and predictability. Routines minimize the uncertainty that can trigger anxiety in children with ADHD, offering a sense of security that comes from knowing what to expect next. This predictability fosters an environment where focus can flourish, as the mental energy once spent on navigating the unpredictable can now be channeled into tasks and learning. The regularity of a well-considered routine also aids in the development of self-discipline and time management skills, foundational competencies that extend far beyond the realm of childhood.

Creating Effective Routines

The crafting of routines that resonate with a child's needs and rhythm is not a task for the faint-hearted. It demands observation, creativity, and, most importantly, iteration. An effective routine starts with the basics—mealtimes, bedtime, and homework—structured around the child's natural peaks and troughs in energy throughout the day. For instance, placing tasks requiring concentration, like homework, during a child's more focused morning hours, while aligning more physical activities to the afternoon can harness their natural cycles of attention and rest. Visual schedules can transform these routines from abstract concepts to tangible guides; think of a chart on the refrigerator door, detailing the day's structure with colorful magnets or stickers to mark transitions. This visual element not only aids in comprehension and memory but also adds an element of fun, encouraging engagement with the routine.

Creating a routine was particularly challenging for me as a partially stay-at-home mom trying to finish my PhD with two toddlers. This structured approach went against my naturally spontaneous nature, but when my ADHD son was about 2.5 years old and we had a new baby, things became exceedingly difficult. The tantrums were frequent, and his anxiety became increasingly evident. To manage this, I worked on establishing daily schedules, especially during the time we were all home due to COVID-19. We would sometimes create the schedule together using a big whiteboard, chunking time and assigning activities. This process was crucial in managing our days, and we noticed a significant reduction in my son's anxiety levels. Having a visual and predictable structure provided him with the stability he needed, making our home environment calmer and more manageable for everyone. We eventually invested in a visual schedule kit that was also something that was very helpful for our family and he enjoyed taking down the pictures of activities as we completed them throughout the day.

Involving Your Child

Involvement in the creation of their routines imbues children with a sense of ownership and control, vital for a demographic often feeling at the mercy of their impulses. This collaboration can start with simple choices, like selecting the sticker that marks homework time on the visual schedule or deciding between two options for the order of morning tasks. Such participation not only increases the likelihood of adherence to the routine but also serves as a practical lesson in decision-making and prioritization.

When we would involve our children in the planning of the schedules or even just the act of setting it up together, we always see greater engagement and adherence. At the end of this chapter is a bonus that walks you through the simple act of how to set up a schedule. You can be as creative or not as you want with this activity. If you have an artist in the house, you could boost engagement by having them decorate the schedule or add color and beauty. There have been times we have done this with poster board and added paint and made it pretty and other times we have used a white board or even a small piece of computer paper. The point is to make it word for you and your ADHD child and try to get them involved in the process.

Flexibility within Structure

The paradox of routines for children with ADHD lies in the necessity for flexibility within the structure. The acknowledgment that some days will diverge from the plan is crucial; a late-night family gathering might extend past bedtime, or an unexpected school assignment may require an adjustment to homework routines. On these days, the routine serves not as a rigid rule but as a flexible guide, one that can adapt to the ebb and flow of life's demands. This adaptability teaches children to manage changes and disruptions without undue stress, cultivating resilience and problem-solving skills. It's about striking a balance, where the routine is respected for its benefits but not adhered to at the cost of well-being or valuable spontaneous experiences.

Strategy Section: Designing Adaptive Routines for Children with ADHD - Routine Creation Guide

Introduction

Managing daily tasks can be particularly challenging for children with ADHD due to their unique needs for structure combined with flexibility. This section presents a guide for parents to collaboratively create and adapt routines with their children, fostering independence while providing the necessary support. We'll explore a practical approach to building morning, after-school, and bedtime routines, complete with visual aids and strategies to accommodate changes.

Step 1: Understanding the Importance of Routine

Children with ADHD benefit significantly from predictable routines that reduce anxiety and decision fatigue. Establishing clear expectations helps these children thrive but maintaining flexibility within those routines is equally crucial to handle the unexpected changes that daily life may bring. This dual focus ensures that routines are helpful rather than restrictive.

Step 2: Collaborative Planning

Engage Your Child: Start by involving your child in the planning process. This inclusion increases their engagement and commitment to following the routine. Discuss what tasks need to be completed and which parts of their current routine are working or not.

Task Identification: With your child, list out the tasks for each part of the day:

- *Morning*: Waking up, getting dressed, eating breakfast, preparing a school bag.
- *After-School*: Completing homework, time for snacks and play, preparing for the next day.
- *Bedtime*: Bathing, teeth brushing, storytime or quiet activity before sleep.

Task Organization: Arrange these tasks in a logical order and discuss how much time each task might realistically take. Allow your child to give input on what feels right for them.

Step 3: Creating the Routine Chart

Design the Chart: Use a large poster board, a digital app, or a large whiteboard to create the routine chart. Assign colors or icons for different types of activities—blue for hygiene, green for meals, and yellow for educational tasks.

Visual Markers: Incorporate visual markers for each task, especially for non-readers. Pictures of a toothbrush or a book can help remind them what comes next without needing to check in with a parent.

Time Estimates: Add a column for time estimates next to each task. Use timers or clocks to help your child keep track of time spent on each activity.

Step 4: Maintaining Flexibility

Adjusting the Routine: Regularly review the routine with your child. Make adjustments as needed, perhaps on a weekly basis, to accommodate changes like extracurricular activities or changes in the school schedule.

Coping with Changes: Discuss how to handle unexpected events. For example, if an after-school appointment might disrupt the routine, talk about how this affects the day and adjust the chart temporarily.

Step 5: Positive Reinforcement and Feedback

Reward System: Implement a reward system for following the routine successfully. Rewards could be stickers on the chart or earning a small privilege like extra playtime or extra evening reading time.

Continuous Feedback: Encourage your child to express how they feel about the routine. This feedback can help refine the process, making the routine more effective and enjoyable for them.

Conclusion

Creating and adapting routines for children with ADHD is not just about structuring their day—it's about empowering them to manage their responsibilities with confidence. This guide provides a foundation for parents to build these essential skills with their children, promoting a sense of security and achievement.

In the whirlwind of life with ADHD, routines aren't just schedules—they're tools that bring some much-needed structure to the day. For kids with ADHD, having a straightforward routine can provide security and make the day more manageable. Establishing routines that focus on consistency, engagement, and flexibility helps kids feel more confident and in control as they move through their day. With some planning, families can create routines that make the unpredictable more stable, allowing for more moments of success, learning, and fun.

These routines do more than keep things running smoothly—they also teach kids essential skills like time management and planning. As they grow, these habits can evolve, helping them navigate the demands of school, friendships, and adult life. By building these routines now, you're creating a more balanced day-to-day and setting your child up with skills they'll carry well into the future.

FLEXIBLE SCHEDULING: ADAPTING TO THE UNPREDICTABLE

In the busy days of raising a child with ADHD, the steady pattern of routine mixes with the unexpected, creating a lifestyle that is both strong and flexible. This duality necessitates a nuanced approach to planning that anticipates variability, ensuring that when the unexpected arrives, it finds a family not besieged by chaos but prepared for adaptation. Creating flexible schedules isn't about getting rid of structure but about adding backup plans into daily routines. This helps families handle unexpected events with ease and confidence.

Planning for Variability

The anticipation of variability begins with an acknowledgment of its inevitability. This recognition informs a planning process that, rather than aspiring to rigid adherence, aims to create a blueprint that accommodates change. Such plans consider the known variables—appointments, school, and work schedules—while leaving spaces open for the unknown, the spontaneous. This might take the form of buffer periods, blocks of time intentionally left unscheduled to absorb the overflow or to provide breathing room for last-minute alterations. It is in these buffers that time becomes a resource rather than a constraint, allowing families to respond to the day's demands without the pressure of an overburdened schedule. Moreover, this approach fosters a mindset that views change not as a disruption to be endured but as an aspect of life to be embraced, teaching children the value of adaptability and resilience.

Time Management Tools

In the arsenal of strategies to navigate the unpredictable, time management tools stand as allies, offering both structure and flexibility. Digital applications designed for task management can serve as invaluable aids, allowing parents and children to visualize the day's commitments and adjust them in real-time. These tools often feature reminders, alerts, and the capacity to share schedules among family members, ensuring that everyone remains informed and in sync. For younger children or for families preferring tactile engagement, physical timers offer a concrete representation of time's passage, making abstract concepts tangible. These can be particularly effective in transitioning between tasks or in delineating the duration of unscheduled periods, providing a clear signal of when it's time to shift focus. The judicious use of these tools, chosen to align with the child's age and preferences, scaffolds the development of time management skills, empowering children with ADHD to navigate their days with increased autonomy and confidence.

Coping with Change

The capacity to cope with change, particularly for a child with ADHD, hinges on the development of strategies that mitigate the stress of the unexpected. This involves not only the child but the family unit, cultivating a collective resilience that can weather the storms of sudden plan alterations. One effective strategy is the practice of scenario planning, a process where parent and child discuss potential changes and devise responses together. These discussions can range from hypothetical situations, such as a rain-canceled outdoor event, to more immediate concerns, like a sudden shift in the day's schedule. This proactive engagement encourages problem-solving and critical thinking, equipping the child with a toolkit of responses that can be accessed when the need arises. Additionally, the practice of mindfulness and grounding techniques, such as deep breathing or sensory engagement exercises, can be invaluable in managing the stress associated with change. By integrating these practices into the daily routine, children learn to anchor themselves in the present, reducing anxiety and enhancing their capacity to adapt to the moment.

Incorporating sensory engagement exercises and mindfulness techniques can significantly bolster a child's ability to handle change. Sensory activities, such as playing with textured materials like sand or slime, can provide a calming effect, helping children stay grounded. Similarly, activities like squeezing a stress ball or using fidget toys can offer a tactile outlet for managing stress. Mindfulness practices, such as deep breathing exercises, can be easily integrated into daily routines. For example, taking a few deep breaths together before starting a new activity can help center and calm your child. Grounding techniques, like the "5-4-3-2-1" exercise, where the child identifies five things they can see, four things they can touch, three things they can hear, two things they can smell, and one thing they can taste, can also help in bringing them back to the present moment. These exercises not only reduce anxiety but also teach children valuable skills for self-regulation and emotional control, making it easier for them to cope with unexpected changes.

Visual Schedules and Reminders

As mentioned in the previous section, the use of visual schedules and reminders plays a pivotal role in bridging the gap between the planned and the unpredictable. These tools transform the abstract concept of time into a visual landscape that children can navigate with ease. A visual schedule, for instance, might depict the day's structure through a series of images or icons, each representing a task or activity. This not only aids in comprehension but also provides a flexible framework that can be adjusted as plans change. Color-coded markers can highlight priorities or denote activities that are fixed versus those that are flexible, offering a quick reference for both parent and child. Similarly, visual reminders, strategically placed in the home or accessed through digital devices, prompt actions or transitions, gently guiding the child through the day's journey. These visual aids serve as anchors, providing consistency and security amidst the fluidity of daily life, enabling children with ADHD to engage with their schedules actively and with a sense of ownership.

In the landscape of parenting a child with ADHD, where the predictable and the unexpected dance is in constant motion, the creation of flexible schedules emerges as both a strategy and a philosophy. It encapsulates an approach to life that values adaptability, embraces change, and empowers children to navigate their world with confidence. Through the intentional design of plans that anticipate variability, the judicious use of time management tools, the cultivation of coping strategies, and the implementation of visual aids, families can transform the unpredictable from a source of stress into an opportunity for growth. This dynamic process, marked by continuous learning and adaptation, not only supports the child in managing the challenges associated with ADHD but also enriches the family's collective experience, weaving a narrative of resilience, flexibility, and unwavering support while building skills that will last a lifetime.

ORGANIZATIONAL SYSTEMS THAT EMPOWER CHILDREN WITH ADHD

In a world where the currents of distraction flow unchecked, the shores of organization offer a haven for minds caught in the tempest of ADHD. Within the sanctum of structure, children find not just the calm after the storm but a launching pad for autonomy and mastery over their environment. This chapter unfolds the layers of organizational skills, methods for managing academic responsibilities, strategies for fostering independence, and the judicious use of reward systems as means to anchor these skills within the daily lives of children with ADHD.

Personal Organization Skills

The quest for personal organization begins in the realms most familiar to the child: their bedroom, study area, and play spaces. In these personal domains, chaos often reigns, not as a sign of disregard but as an external manifestation of internal disarray. The strategy here involves more than mere tidying; it encompasses teaching the child to classify, categorize, and maintain their environment through systems that resonate with their unique way of processing the world. This might involve color-coded systems for clothing, transparent bins for toys, or designated zones within a room that delineate areas for study, rest, and play. Engaging the child in the creation of these systems ensures that they hold meaning and relevance, transforming the act of organization from a chore into a personalized expression of their space. Digital tools, too, lend their might, offering apps that gamify the organization process or provide visual reminders to declutter and reorganize, bridging the gap between the physical and virtual realms of the child's world.

Homework and School Projects

The battleground of homework and school projects, where deadlines loom and distractions abound, demands a tactical approach to foster success without stress. Here, the introduction of a project planner, whether in a digital format that sends reminders or a physical planner that allows for the tangible tracking of progress, serves as a compass guiding the child through the maze of assignments. Breaking down large tasks into manageable segments, each with its own mini-deadline, allows the child to navigate academic responsibilities with clear waypoints, reducing the overwhelm that often accompanies expansive projects. The environment, too, plays a critical role; a dedicated homework station, free from the siren calls of unrelated gadgets and toys, focuses the mind, transforming the space into a cocoon of concentration. Through these methods, the child learns to approach academic tasks not as insurmountable mountains but as a series of manageable hills, where each climb brings its own sense of achievement and mastery.

Empowering Independence

The core of organizational skills lies in their power to foster independence, to shift the child from dependency on external prompts to the self-guided navigation of their day. This evolution begins with simple tasks that embed autonomy into the fabric of daily life. A morning checklist, for instance, empowers the child to ready themselves for school without constant supervision, instilling a sense of pride and capability. Similarly as discussed previously, involving the child in planning their week, from extracurricular activities to family outings, teaches them to anticipate and prepare for upcoming events, weaving time management into the toolbox of their skill set. Technology, too, offers a scaffold for this growth, with timers and apps that remind the child of tasks with autonomy rather than authority, nudging rather than pushing them towards their responsibilities. As these skills solidify, the child discovers the joy in self-reliance, in the knowledge that they can steer their ship through the day's demands with confidence and skill.

Reward Systems

In the narrative of organizational growth, reward systems emerge not as mere incentives but as acknowledgments of effort and progress, milestones that mark the journey of mastering organizational skills. These systems thrive on specificity and immediacy, where rewards are directly tied to observable actions and are granted soon after the accomplishment. A sticker chart, for instance, might track the days when the child successfully follows their morning routine, culminating in a chosen activity or privilege at the week's end. Digital badges or points can serve a similar purpose for older children, offering virtual recognition for tasks completed or goals met. Yet, the most potent rewards often lie in the realm of the intangible; verbal praise, shared moments of joy, and the visible pride in a parent's eyes. These rewards, unquantifiable yet invaluable, weave a deeper motivation into the child's heart, driving them towards not just external rewards but the intrinsic satisfaction that comes from a challenge met and a job well done.

In the crafting of organizational systems that empower children with ADHD, the aim extends beyond the mere imposition of order. It seeks to instill a sense of mastery, autonomy, and pride in the child, to equip them with the skills to navigate not just their personal spaces but the broader academic and social landscapes of their lives. Through personalized strategies that resonate with the child's unique needs and perspectives, the integration of technology as a tool for engagement and autonomy, and the thoughtful application of reward systems that celebrate progress, children with ADHD discover not just the calm within the storm but the ability to chart their course through it, organized, confident, and independent.

BALANCING STRUCTURE WITH SPONTANEITY: FAMILY TIME REDEFINED

Finding time to connect is crucial in the busy rhythm of family life, especially for families dealing with the ups and downs of ADHD. These shared moments are more than just time together—they're opportunities to build stronger bonds and create lasting memories. For families like ours, these moments provide stability and connection amid the daily chaos.

Planning family time isn't just about putting something on the calendar; it's about striking the right balance between having a routine and allowing flexibility. Some days, it might mean sticking to a favorite family game night or outing, while other times, it's about embracing spur-of-the-moment fun. The goal is to create an environment where everyone feels included and valued, no matter their unique needs or personalities. By finding this balance, you create space where everyone can thrive, explore, and, most importantly, connect with one another.

Quality Family Time

The quest for quality in the time families spend together often leads down paths less trodden, away from the glare of screens and the din of digital distractions. Activities grounded in the tactile and the tangible offer a richer array of experiences, allowing for engagement that is both meaningful and mindful. Consider the simple act of preparing a meal together, where each task, from chopping vegetables to setting the table, becomes a lesson in teamwork and a chance for conversation. For a child with ADHD, these activities also serve as opportunities to practice focus and follow-through in a nurturing environment. Similarly, outdoor excursions, be it to a local park or a nature trail, invite exploration and stimulate the senses in ways that indoor environments seldom can. Here, amid the rustle of leaves and the whispers of the wind, families find a shared ground, a place where the frenetic pace of daily life gives way to the rhythms of nature, encouraging presence and participation from all.

Spontaneous Adventures

The infusion of spontaneity into family life acts as a catalyst for joy, an invitation to embrace the unexpected with open arms. Spontaneous adventures, unplanned and unstructured, spark creativity and a sense of wonder, reminding each member of the beauty inherent in the unpredictable. These adventures need not be grandiose or far-flung; they can be as simple as a surprise picnic in the backyard or an impromptu art session on a rainy afternoon. For children with ADHD, these breaks from routine are not just welcome diversions but essential outlets for their boundless energy and creativity. They serve as reminders that while structure provides a necessary scaffold for managing ADHD, freedom and flexibility are equally vital in nurturing the spirit and sparking the imagination.

Individual and Group Activities

In family life, everyone brings something unique to the table. Balancing both individual and group activities helps everyone feel valued and connected. Encouraging personal interests and hobbies gives each family member a sense of identity and confidence. These individual pursuits aren't just about alone time—they offer a chance for self-expression and growth. And when family members share what they've been working on or learning, it creates moments of connection and mutual respect.

Conversely, group activities—like game nights, outdoor adventures, or even shared projects—strengthen family bonds through shared experiences. Finding activities that everyone enjoys helps build a sense of togetherness. It reinforces the joy that comes from spending time as a family. By mixing individual pursuits with group fun, you're supporting each person's growth and bringing everyone closer together in a meaningful way.

Celebrating Small Wins

In family life, especially when dealing with the ups and downs of ADHD, celebrating victories—both big and small—can have a considerable impact. Recognizing the effort and progress behind each win strengthens positive connections within the family and boosts everyone's sense of belonging. For a child with ADHD, these celebrations are more than just moments of praise—they're affirmations of their strengths and contributions, helping to counterbalance any feelings of struggle or frustration they might experience.

It's important to celebrate the small wins, too, like sticking to a routine, finishing homework independently, or having a conflict-free day. These moments deserve acknowledgment, whether it's through a special treat, a family game night, or even a heartfelt compliment. By making these achievements a big deal, you're reinforcing positive behaviors and creating lasting memories that highlight the progress and growth within your family. These celebrations help build a more encouraging environment where every effort is recognized and appreciated.

In our family, we make a point to celebrate the little victories in meaningful ways. I remember when my son managed to stay on top of his daily checklist for an entire week—something that was a big deal for him. We made a big fuss with a special "choose your own dinner" night where he picked the menu and got to be the "chef" for the evening. Another time, when my other son, who usually has a hard time with transitions, breezed through his morning routine without any hiccups, we surprised him with a spontaneous trip to his favorite ice cream spot. These moments aren't just about the treats—they're about showing our kids that their efforts, no matter how small, are noticed and appreciated. These celebrations help reinforce the message that hard work and progress are worth acknowledging and can be fun, too!

Finding the right balance between structure and spontaneity in family life is vital to supporting everyone's needs while allowing room for growth. Whether planned activities or last-minute adventures, making time for both helps strengthen your family's connection. It's about creating moments that let each person shine individually while bringing everyone together. Recognizing and celebrating each small step forward, no matter how minor, is a testament to your family's progress and fosters a deep sense of belonging.

This approach, rooted in flexibility, empathy, and celebrating each other's efforts, doesn't just make day-to-day life smoother—it sets the stage for a future where everyone feels valued and empowered. By blending routine with a willingness to adapt, you create a family environment where each member can thrive, knowing they're supported and appreciated. This empowerment is a testament to your effective parenting.

Shifting our gaze forward, we turn to the realms of social skills and relationship-building, essential areas where the principles of understanding, empathy, and intentional engagement continue to guide the way.

CHAPTER 4
EMBRACING THE SPECTRUM: A STRENGTH-BASED APPROACH TO ADHD

Every child with ADHD has their own unique strengths, even if those strengths aren't always immediately visible. Instead of focusing on their struggles, a strength-based approach highlights what they're good at and what makes them shine. This shift in perspective allows their abilities to take center stage, giving them the recognition and support they need to thrive.

By focusing on what they naturally excel at—creativity, problem-solving, or a knack for thinking outside the box—you help your child build confidence and feel valued for who they are. This approach boosts self-esteem and sets the stage for personal growth. It's about creating an environment where their strengths are acknowledged, giving them the space to develop those talents while also working on the challenges that come with ADHD. When we prioritize strengths, we're not just managing the diagnosis—we're helping our kids genuinely flourish.

HIGHLIGHTING STRENGTHS: A NEW PERSPECTIVE ON ADHD

Identifying Unique Strengths

Discovering a child's unique strengths begins with observation and a keen eye tuned to moments of engagement, joy, and success. Every day, from a child's meticulous construction of a Lego tower to their captivating storytelling, these gems of ability glimmer. A systematic approach involves maintaining a strengths journal, a dedicated space where parents note instances of creativity, problem-solving, empathy, or any skill their child demonstrates. This practice serves as a repository of positive attributes and a tool for shifting focus from challenges to capabilities, offering a tangible reminder of the child's potential.

Teachers can contribute to this endeavor through specific feedback, highlighting moments when a child's strengths shine. Whether their innovative approach to a project or their leadership during group activities, these insights provide a broader view of the child's abilities, reinforcing the strengths observed at home.

Reframing ADHD

Changing the narrative around ADHD from limitation to potential requires a paradigm shift, where the traits often labeled as disruptive are seen through a lens of possibility. Hyperfocus, for instance, transforms into a powerful tool for deep exploration and mastery of subjects that capture the child's interest. When channeled appropriately, impulsivity becomes spontaneity and bravery in trying new things. This reframing is not a dismissal of ADHD's challenges but an expansion of the narrative to include the full spectrum of the child's experience, highlighting their capacity for innovation, resilience, and empathy.

In conversations with educators, parents, and peers, this perspective encourages a more holistic understanding of ADHD, promoting strategies that leverage these strengths in both academic and social settings. It's a dialogue that fosters an inclusive environment where children feel valued for who they are, not despite their ADHD but inclusive of it.

Success Stories

Inspirational stories of individuals who have harnessed their ADHD traits for success serve as powerful beacons of possibility. From entrepreneurs who credit their innovative thinking to ADHD to artists whose boundless creativity is fueled by their unique neurological wiring, these narratives offer tangible proof of the potential within a strength-based approach. Sharing these stories with children expands their view of what is possible. It instills a sense of pride and belonging, reinforcing that ADHD is not a barrier to success but a different path to achieving it.

Workshops, speaker series, books, or family discussions featuring individuals or characters with ADHD who have found success in various fields provide relatable models for children. These encounters illuminate the diverse ways ADHD traits can be assets, encouraging children to explore and embrace their unique talents.

Positive Affirmations

The power of language in shaping self-perception is profound. Positive affirmations, tailored to celebrate the individual strengths of a child with ADHD, are daily reminders of their worth and potential. Phrases like "Your creativity knows no bounds" or "Your enthusiasm brings so much joy" reinforce the child's sense of self-worth, counteracting any negative narratives they may encounter. These affirmations can be integrated into daily routines, displayed in the child's living spaces, or included in notes tucked into lunchboxes, offering consistent, uplifting messages that bolster the child's self-esteem.

Strategy Section: Strength-Based Journal Prompts

A strengths-based journal can provide a structured yet flexible way for parents and children to document and reflect on the child's abilities and successes. This journal could include prompts to guide observations, spaces for date and details of the strength observed, and sections for photos or drawings that capture moments of achievement. By regularly updating this journal, families create a living document that celebrates the child's growth and talents, serving as a source of encouragement and a tool for advocacy in discussions with educators and support professionals. The next section provides some journal prompts that can begin this valuable process. If your child is resistant, you could also use these as conversation prompts and begin the journal for your child.

To begin and enrich the strength-based journal, here are some prompts designed to help parents and children focus on positive aspects of their day and recognize their unique abilities. These prompts encourage reflection and provide a structured way to highlight strengths and successes.

Daily Wins

- What is something you did today that you are proud of?
- Describe a moment today when you felt happy or accomplished. What were you doing?

Strength Spotlight

- What is one of your strengths that you used today? How did it help you?
- Think of a time when you helped someone else today. What did you do, and how did it make you feel?

Challenges and Solutions

- Describe a challenge you faced today. How did you overcome it?
- What is something you learned from a mistake today? How can you use this lesson in the future?

Creative Expressions

- Draw or describe something you created today. Why does it make you proud?

- Write a short story or draw a picture about a superhero who has the same strengths as you.

Gratitude Moments

- What is something you are grateful for today? How did it make your day better?
- Who is someone you appreciate in your life, and why?

By regularly engaging with these prompts, children can develop a habit of recognizing and celebrating their strengths, while parents can gain valuable insights into their child's growth and areas of confidence. This practice not only boosts self-esteem but also provides a rich resource for understanding and supporting the child's unique journey.

ACTIVITIES THAT SHOWCASE YOUR CHILD'S UNIQUE ABILITIES

Selecting extracurricular activities that resonate with a child's innate strengths and curiosities can transform an ordinary after-school program or hobby into a vibrant arena where self-discovery and growth unfold. When embarking on this selection, consider not just the appeal of an activity but its alignment with the child's natural inclinations and talents. Is there a fascination with how things work that could be nurtured through robotics? Does a love for storytelling suggest drama or creative writing clubs? This matching process is not about projecting ambitions onto the child but offering pathways that amplify their passions and abilities. Engage the child in this decision-making, discussing options and observing their reactions, ensuring the chosen activities feel like adventures they are eager to undertake, not obligations they must fulfill.

I remember when my son showed an interest in sports. Knowing that baseball would likely be too slow-paced for him, we opted for soccer, a more engaging and high-energy sport that really matched his energy. The moment he stepped onto the field, he was in his element, running around and fully immersed in the game. It was the perfect outlet for his boundless energy. Similarly, when we noticed his love for music, we explored music therapy. Watching him connect with rhythm and melody during sessions was incredible—it wasn't just an activity, it was a joyful and therapeutic experience that tapped into his passion. These experiences have not only helped him develop new skills but also boosted his confidence, as he discovered new aspects of himself he didn't know existed.

The realm of creativity and innovation offers fertile ground for children with ADHD, whose minds often teem with ideas that defy conventional boundaries. Encouraging this creative expression requires more than just providing the tools for art, music, or writing; it involves creating an atmosphere where originality is celebrated and "mistakes" are viewed as steps in the creative process. Facilitate environments at home where experimentation is encouraged, whether through impromptu jam sessions with instruments, a wall dedicated to mural painting, or a tech corner for coding projects. These spaces become laboratories for imaginative exploration, where children can translate their whirlwind of thoughts into tangible creations, affirming their creative capacities and enhancing their ability to concentrate and see projects through to completion.

At home, we experienced this firsthand when our ADHD child became engrossed in learning all about big ships when he was in 2nd grade, especially the Titanic and other famous shipwrecks. During this phase, he was obsessed with experimenting by making boats out of tin foil and testing their buoyancy in the bathroom sink or bathtub. My husband and I had to fight our natural inclination for order and cleanliness and let him "waste" some tin foil in his experiments. Watching him meticulously craft his boats and eagerly test them was a joy, despite the occasional mess. This period of experimentation not only fueled his curiosity and creativity but also provided him with a hands-on learning experience that enhanced his problem-solving skills and deepened his engagement with a subject he was passionate about. It reminded us of the importance of embracing the chaos that sometimes comes with nurturing creativity, allowing our child the freedom to explore and learn in his unique way.

Physical activities and sports, often recommended for their health benefits, hold particular significance for children with ADHD, offering channels for surplus energy and arenas for developing focus and discipline. Yet, selecting a sport or physical activity should pivot on the child's enjoyment and sense of achievement rather than on competitiveness or the pursuit of excellence. Activities that blend physical exertion with elements of strategy and teamwork, such as soccer, basketball, or martial arts, can be particularly beneficial. These environments teach children the value of persistence, the importance of following rules, and the satisfaction of contributing to a team's efforts. Moreover, the structure provided by regular practices and the immediate feedback inherent in physical activities helps in setting clear goals and understanding the steps needed to achieve them, reinforcing discipline in a context that feels rewarding.

Family projects offer a unique canvas for showcasing and nurturing the diverse abilities of each family member, creating a collective masterpiece that reflects the contributions of all. These projects could range from building a backyard garden, where planning, patience, and care yield tangible rewards, to undertaking a DIY home improvement project, blending creativity with practical skills. In these shared endeavors, children with ADHD can take on roles that play to their strengths, whether that's in brainstorming designs, leading the execution, or adding artistic touches. The key lies in framing these projects as collaborative efforts, where each task is vital to success, no matter how small. This collaborative approach bolsters the child's sense of belonging and significance within the family. It provides practical lessons in teamwork, responsibility, and the gratification of seeing an idea come to life.

Through the deliberate selection of activities that echo a child's interests and abilities, the promotion of creative and innovative expression, the incorporation of physical activities that enhance focus and self-esteem, and the undertaking of family projects that celebrate collaborative achievement, children with ADHD are offered avenues to shine. These experiences, rich in learning and self-discovery, underscore the child's potential not just to cope with ADHD but to excel, transforming perceived obstacles into stepping stones of growth. In these activities, every child finds their stage. Their talents are displayed and revered in this place, where their contributions are accepted and needed. This approach is firmly rooted in the unique blend of each child's abilities and passions.It weaves a narrative where ADHD is merely one thread in the vibrant mosaic of their identity, contributing depth and texture to the unfolding story of their lives.

FOSTERING A GROWTH MINDSET IN YOUR NEURODIVERSE CHILD

Neurodiversity, with its wide range of talents and challenges, is a fertile ground for fostering a growth mindset. Rather than viewing abilities as fixed, a growth mindset instills the belief that skills and strengths can evolve through dedication and perseverance. This shift in perspective can be a beacon of hope for parents, educators, and caregivers of kids with ADHD. It redirects the focus from limitations to the potential for growth and improvement, instilling a sense of optimism and empowerment.

In practice, this means that parents and educators play a crucial role in helping children with ADHD understand that setbacks are part of learning and that progress is made step by step. By embracing this mindset, kids with ADHD can build resilience and gain confidence in overcoming obstacles. It's about fostering a belief that they can keep improving and that hard work pays off, turning perceived limitations into opportunities for personal growth. Your role is pivotal in this journey, empowering you to make a significant difference in their lives.

Psychologist Carol Dweck introduced the idea of a growth mindset, which is the belief that intelligence and skills aren't fixed—they can grow with effort, good strategies, and the proper support. For a child with ADHD, adopting this mindset can be a game-changer. It helps them see challenges not as roadblocks but as opportunities to learn and improve. Instead of getting stuck on what they're naturally good at, a growth mindset encourages them to focus on persistence, effort, and the courage to keep going when things get tough. It's all about shifting the focus from "What can't I do?" to "How can I get better at this?"

Viewing challenges as opportunities for growth necessitates reorienting how success and failure are perceived. It involves guiding your child to see beyond a setback's immediate frustration, peel back the layers, and uncover the learning hidden within. This process might include sitting beside them as they tackle homework, not to provide answers but to encourage them to approach problems from different angles, to try and fail and try again, each attempt shedding light on new thinking pathways. It's about highlighting the progress made, no matter how small, and framing each challenge as a question: "What can we learn from this?"

Encouraging persistence in the face of setbacks becomes a daily practice, a series of moments where encouragement meets action. It can be as simple as verbal reminders of past successes when faced with a new challenge or as involved as setting up a "persistence project" that requires sustained effort over time, celebrating each small victory along the way. This persistence is nurtured through words and actions that demonstrate faith in their capabilities, such as providing opportunities for independence and responsibility that stretch their skills and self-belief.

Celebrating effort over outcome fundamentally alters the reward landscape for a child with ADHD, placing the emphasis on the journey rather than the destination. It means applauding the hours spent on a project and the concentration battled for and achieved, even if the result isn't perfect. It's recognizing the bravery in asking for help and the resilience in trying again after a mistake. Such celebrations can be woven into the fabric of daily life, from reflective conversations about what was learned in tackling a day's tasks to creating a visual "effort tracker" that highlights the process rather than the product.

This cultivation of a growth mindset within the neurodiverse landscape of ADHD does not deny the challenges inherent in the condition. Still, it reframes them as part of a larger narrative of growth and learning. It recognizes that each child's journey is unique, with its obstacles and triumphs. Still, it underscores a universal truth: within every challenge lies an opportunity for development, expanding the boundaries of what is possible. Through a consistent focus on growth, resilience, and the celebration of effort, children with ADHD learn not just to navigate their world with greater confidence but to reshape it with their unique talents and perspectives.

NEURODIVERSITY AND IDENTITY: CONVERSATIONS WITH YOUR CHILD

Talking to your child about neurodiversity and ADHD can be a powerful way to help them understand and accept who they are. These conversations give your child the chance to see ADHD not as something that makes them "different" in a negative way but as a critical part of who they are. The goal is to make these discussions straightforward and relatable, avoiding confusing medical terms and focusing on what neurodiversity means—the idea that everyone's brain works a little differently, and that's not just okay, it's completely normal.

Explaining ADHD within the bigger picture of neurodiversity helps your child see that, just like people have different strengths and weaknesses, our brains have unique ways of working. You can use simple stories or examples they can connect with, such as a puzzle with different shapes and sizes, or a garden with diverse flowers and plants, helping them understand that there's no "right" or "wrong" way to think or learn. By framing ADHD in this broader context, you're not just educating them—you're giving them the tools to feel confident in their identity and to embrace how they experience the world.

Building a positive identity in the context of ADHD and neurodiversity involves nurturing a child's self-perception that is anchored in acceptance and pride rather than shame or inadequacy. This undertaking starts with acknowledging ADHD's challenges while emphasizing the child's strengths and capabilities. Encouraging children to explore and define their interests, talents, and dreams contributes to a comprehensive self-image grounded in reality. This process is bolstered by language that celebrates diversity and resilience, painting ADHD as one of many threads in the tapestry of their identity that adds depth, color, and texture.

Addressing and dismantling the stigma associated with ADHD and neurodiversity calls for a twofold approach: equipping children with factual information to counteract myths and fostering environments where open discussions about ADHD are normalized. Parents and caregivers can model how to respond to misinformed comments or stereotypes, offering language children can use to advocate for themselves and educate others. This empowerment extends beyond the family. It encourages children to engage in peer discussions, school projects, and social media platforms to share their perspectives, contributing to a broader cultural shift towards acceptance and understanding.

Empowering children to advocate for themselves and others is critical in cultivating a sense of agency and belonging. This empowerment begins with small, everyday actions—choosing when to disclose their ADHD, requesting accommodations, or expressing their needs and preferences. As children mature, these advocacy skills include standing up for peers, participating in awareness campaigns, or engaging in community projects promoting neurodiversity. Through advocacy, children assert their place in the world and join a more significant movement that champions diversity and inclusion.

By navigating these conversations and experiences, children with ADHD embark on a journey towards self-acceptance, armed with the understanding that their unique way of interacting with the world adds invaluable depth to the human mosaic. Parents play a crucial role in facilitating discussions and creating supportive environments encouraging their children to embrace and celebrate their neurodiversity, recognizing it as a source of strength, creativity, and resilience.

I remember the first time I really engaged with my son about his ADHD. He was only seven, but he found an ADHD superhero workbook meant for older children and couldn't stop devouring it. He was so curious about what it meant for him, flipping through the pages and asking endless questions. The relief on his face as we talked was unforgettable. He seemed to light up with the realization that his ADHD was not a burden but a unique part of who he was. This experience underscored for me the importance of maintaining an open dialogue. It showed how powerful it is to create a space where children feel safe to explore and understand their neurodiversity, helping them see it as a source of strength rather than a limitation.

When we talk openly about neurodiversity, build a positive sense of identity, address stigma, and encourage self-advocacy, we start to reshape the story around ADHD. Instead of seeing it as a limitation, we can help our kids embrace it as an essential part of their identity. Every child, no matter their neurodiversity, has value and potential. By having honest conversations, providing consistent support, and teaching them to speak up for themselves, we give them the confidence to see their ADHD as a strength rather than a setback.

Moving forward, focusing on acceptance, understanding, and empowerment becomes critical. These principles help our kids navigate the world with confidence and pave the way for a future where neurodiversity is celebrated as an essential part of what makes each of us unique.

CHAPTER 5
TRANSFORMING TURMOIL INTO TRANQUILITY

Parenting a child with ADHD often involves dealing with sudden outbursts that can quickly throw the whole household into chaos. These intense moments can leave parents scrambling to figure out how to restore calm. But there's also a chance to learn and grow within these challenging situations. This chapter focuses on understanding what triggers these outbursts and offers practical, effective strategies to help you anticipate and manage them. By identifying the root causes and using these effective techniques, you can shift from reacting to these situations to creating a more peaceful environment, empowering you to take control.

UNDERSTANDING THE TRIGGERS OF EXPLOSIVE BEHAVIOR

Identifying Triggers

Understanding what sets off explosive behavior in children with ADHD requires careful observation and attention to detail, much like a detective looking for clues. Triggers can vary widely—from the frustration of breaking a routine to the sensory overload of a noisy environment. The first step is to closely monitor your child's behavior and surroundings, looking for patterns that tend to lead to outbursts. For example, do they get overwhelmed in crowded malls or birthday parties? Are meltdowns more common at a particular time of day, like late afternoons, when energy is low? By keeping track of these patterns, you can better anticipate what might set them off and develop strategies to avoid or manage these triggers before they escalate.

Trigger Patterns

Keeping a detailed record of your child's behavior and the situations leading up to it can be incredibly helpful in spotting patterns. Over time, this log gives you insights to better predict and manage potential outbursts. For example, you might notice that transitions between activities often trigger meltdowns, signaling the need for more structured and gradual changes. You may also find that issues tend to arise in the late afternoon, which could point to tiredness or hunger as contributing factors. By tracking these patterns, you can proactively address triggers and create strategies to reduce the chances of outbursts. This sense of accomplishment in creating effective strategies can bring a satisfying feeling of success, making daily life smoother for everyone.

Sensory Overloads

For many children with ADHD, sensory overstimulation serves as a significant trigger for explosive behavior. The relentless assault of bright lights, loud noises, or even the texture of clothing can escalate from discomfort to distress in moments. Understanding this, parents can become adept at reading the signs of sensory overwhelm and intervening before it reaches a tipping point. Strategies include:

- Providing noise-canceling headphones during outings.
- Choosing clothing made of soft, non-irritating materials.
- Creating a quiet retreat space at home where the child can decompress away from sensory stimuli.

Emotional Underpinnings

At the heart of many explosive behaviors lie unmet emotional needs or frustrations. A child's inability to articulate sadness, fear, or insecurity can manifest as anger or defiance. Diving into these emotional undercurrents requires patience, empathy, and open lines of communication. Encouraging the child to express feelings through words, art, or play can offer insights into their emotional world, uncovering the root causes of behavior. This understanding allows parents to address the underlying needs through reassurance, problem-solving, or simply offering a listening ear, reducing the frequency and intensity of outbursts.

Strategy Section: Implementing a Trigger Tracking Log

For parents of children with ADHD, understanding the root causes of explosive behaviors is a key step in managing and mitigating these challenging moments. One effective tool for this purpose is a Trigger Tracking Journal. This journal offers a structured way to document and analyze your child's behavior patterns, providing valuable insights into what triggers outbursts and how to address them proactively.

How to Create a Trigger Tracking Journal

1. Choose a Format:

- Physical Journal: A notebook with divided sections or a binder with pre-made templates can work well.
- Digital Journal: An Excel spreadsheet, a note-taking app, or a specific behavior-tracking app can also be effective for those who prefer to keep everything on their devices.

2. Set Up Your Journal:

Columns/Sections to Include:

- Date and Time: Note when the outburst or challenging behavior occurs.
- Location: Record where the behavior took place (e.g., home, school, playground).

- Activity Before the Outburst: Describe what your child was doing just before the incident.
- Possible Triggers: List any potential triggers, such as loud noises, transitions, frustration, or unexpected changes.
- Emotional and Physical State: Observe and note your child's mood, energy level, hunger, or other physical factors.
- Notes/Outcome: Reflect on how the situation was handled, what worked, what didn't, and any immediate aftermath or resolution.

3. Implement the Journal:

- Consistency is Key: Make it a habit to record relevant incidents as soon as possible after they occur. Consistent documentation over several weeks will provide a clearer picture of patterns and triggers.
- Involve the Child: Depending on their age and understanding, you might involve your child in the process by discussing the entries and reflecting together on what may have caused the outburst. This can foster self-awareness and help your child start recognizing their own triggers.

Analyzing and Using the Data

1. Look for Patterns:

- After a few weeks of diligent tracking, review the journal to identify common triggers or settings that

seem to precede challenging behaviors.
- Notice any recurring emotional or physical states, such as fatigue or hunger, that might be contributing factors.

2. Develop Strategies:

- Use the insights gained from the journal to create personalized strategies for avoiding or mitigating triggers. For example, if transitions from playtime to homework often lead to outbursts, a strategy might involve introducing a 10-minute warning with a calm-down activity to ease the transition.
- Share your findings with teachers or other caregivers to ensure consistency in managing triggers across different environments.

3. Monitor Progress:

- Continue using the journal to track the effectiveness of new strategies. Adjust as necessary, celebrating successes and refining approaches when needed.

A Real-Life Example:

When our ADHD child was about 2.5 years old, we noticed that his anxiety and tantrums were often linked to unexpected changes in his routine. During the COVID-19 lockdown, we implemented a daily schedule using a big whiteboard, where we would chunk time and assign activities together. This visual aid helped reduce his anxiety, as he could see what was coming next and feel more in control.

We noticed a significant improvement in his behavior once we understood his triggers and made adjustments to prevent or better manage them.

The Trigger Tracking Journal can be a powerful tool in your parenting toolkit, transforming potential points of conflict into opportunities for growth and understanding. By taking the time to observe, record, and reflect, you can gain a deeper understanding of your child's unique needs and responses, ultimately fostering a more peaceful and supportive environment for everyone.

Calming Techniques for Immediate Use During Meltdowns

In the labyrinth of parenting a child with ADHD, navigating the sudden storms of meltdowns demands not only patience and understanding but a toolkit equipped with strategies that can soothe and stabilize. These moments, fraught with intense emotion and distress, challenge parents to apply immediate calming techniques that can gently steer the child back to equilibrium. Within this crucible of crisis, the application of breathing exercises, the creation of safe spaces, the utilization of sensory tools, and the employment of verbal cues emerge as pillars upon which tranquility can be restored.

Balloon and Square Breathing and Hot Cocoa Breaths

Breathing exercises, often overlooked in their simplicity, have a profound ability to bring both child and caregiver back to the present moment, helping to calm the chaos of a meltdown with the steady rhythm of inhaling and exhaling. Teaching a child to focus on their breath takes practice, and it's most effective when introduced during moments of calm to prepare for times of stress. One effective technique is "balloon breathing." In this exercise, the child imagines filling their belly with air, just like inflating a balloon. As they take a deep breath in, their belly expands, and the balloon fills up. Then, they slowly exhale, emptying the balloon and pulling their belly in and chest down as if the balloon is gently deflating. Practicing this together not only teaches your child how to regain control in stressful situations but also creates a shared ritual that reinforces their sense of security and connection.

Another technique, referred to here as square breathing is a simple yet powerful technique that can help children with ADHD manage their anxiety and regain focus. To practice square breathing, have your child trace a box in the air with their finger. As they trace up one side of the box, they should slowly inhale for a count of four. When they reach the top, they hold their breath for another count of four as they trace across the top of the box. Then, they exhale slowly along the other side of the box, counting to four again, and finally hold their breath at the bottom for four counts before starting the cycle over. This rhythmic breathing pattern can help calm the nervous system and bring your child back to the present moment.

Another engaging technique is the "hot cocoa breaths" exercise, introduced by Dr. Becky Kennedy in her book *Good Inside*. In this exercise, encourage your child to imagine holding a warm mug of hot cocoa. They start by "smelling" the cocoa, taking a deep inhale through the nose as if they're savoring the rich chocolate aroma. Then, they slowly exhale through their mouth as if they're blowing gently on the cocoa to cool it down, like blowing through a straw, being careful not to blow the marshmallows off the top. This visualization makes the exercise fun and relatable, turning a simple breath control technique into a calming ritual that children can use anytime they need to manage their emotions or find focus.

Breathing exercises play a crucial role in regulating the nervous system, particularly for children with ADHD. By focusing on the breath, we can activate the body's parasympathetic nervous system, which helps to calm the "fight or flight" response and bring a sense of peace and stability. This shift allows both the mind and body to settle, reducing feelings of anxiety and overwhelm. Regular practice of mindful breathing not only equips children with a powerful tool to manage their emotions but also helps to create a foundation of resilience, enabling them to navigate the challenges of daily life with greater ease and confidence.

Space and Sensory Tools

Establishing a safe space within the home acts as a sanctuary to which a child can retreat, a tactile haven insulated from the triggers and tumult of the external world. This space, personalized to the child's comfort and preferences, might be adorned with soft pillows, favorite toys, or items that provide a tactile sense of security, such as a beloved blanket. The key lies in its designation as a voluntary retreat. In this place, the child can self-regulate without the perception of isolation or punishment. Creating such a space involves the child in its design, ensuring it resonates as a personal cocoon, reflective of their needs and soothing to their senses.

Sensory tools, tailored to the individual's unique sensory profile, offer a tangible means for children to navigate back to calm. Stress balls, when squeezed, provide a physical outlet for the release of tension, the act of compression and release mirroring the psychological journey from distress to composure. Weighted blankets, draped over the shoulders or lap, can simulate the reassuring pressure of a hug, its weight signaling the nervous system to shift from states of alertness to relaxation. Fidget toys, manipulated by restless hands, can be a focal point for dissipating energy, allowing the child's mind to transition from a state of overstimulation to one of focused calm. The selection and introduction of these tools to the child's repertoire are guided by attentive observation of their responses, ensuring each tool's efficacy in providing comfort and stability.

Verbal cues, employed with sensitivity and consistency, become verbal anchors, drawing the child back from the brink of emotional overflow. These cues, simple phrases or words chosen in collaboration with the child, signal a shared understanding and a call to the established regulation techniques, such as breathing exercises or retreat to the safe space. "Remember our balloon," whispered gently, can remind the child of their breathing exercises. At the same time "Let's find your calm," spoken softly or "relax your body," can guide them towards their safe space or sensory tool. The effectiveness of these cues rests in their repetition and the calm, reassuring tone in which they are delivered, serving not as commands but as invitations to engage in self-soothing practices.

In this intricate dance of de-escalation, where each step from breathing exercises to the utilization of verbal cues is measured and mindful, the goal transcends mere cessation of the immediate meltdown. It seeks to instill in the child a sense of agency over their emotions, a toolkit of techniques they can draw upon in distress. This empowerment, cultivated through practice, patience, and the consistent application of calming strategies, offers a lifeline in the storm of a meltdown and a foundation upon which resilience and self-regulation can be built. Through these efforts, parents and caregivers create a network of support, each part representing a technique or tool that surrounds the child with understanding and equips them to navigate their emotional world with increased competence and confidence.

Personal Tools

In our house, we had a secret weapon for those moments of extreme chaos or sensory overload—a cocoon compression swing. Whenever things got a bit too hectic, we'd set up the swing, pop in some books and stuffed animals, and one by one let the kids take a breather. We'd set a timer and let them chill out in their cozy little hideaway. This was a lifesaver, especially when our oldest started kindergarten. Every morning after breakfast, he'd get some swing time before catching the bus. It helped him start the day feeling calm and ready to tackle whatever came his way.

Another tool we discovered was all about hanging upside down. We noticed our oldest would watch TV while hanging upside down off the couch, and it seemed to have a calming effect on him. So, we decided to use this to our advantage. After a tantrum, we'd encourage him to hang off his bed for a bit. It turned out to be a great calming tactic, helping him to relax and reset. This simple trick became a go-to method for managing meltdowns and finding a bit of peace in those hectic moments.

Understanding what triggers your child's behavior is crucial, but equally important is knowing the calming techniques and tricks that work best for them. Every child is different, and what soothes one might not work for another. In our home, the cocoon compression swing and the upside-down hanging trick became essential tools in our parenting toolkit. These strategies helped our oldest navigate their emotions and provided us with a way to bring calm to the chaos. By identifying and using these calming techniques, we were able to create a more peaceful and supportive environment for our children.

POST-MELTDOWN CONVERSATIONS: HEALING AND LEARNING

In the aftermath of the storm, when the air still vibrates with the echoes of a meltdown, the terrain becomes ripe for seeds of understanding and growth. The period following an emotional outburst holds an invaluable opportunity for connection, reflection, and empowerment within its fragile moments. In this tender afterglow of tempest, parents find the delicate task of engaging in conversations that aim not to reprimand but to understand, not to lecture but to learn together with their child.

Timing for Talks

Navigating the delicate timing for initiating these discussions demands an attunement to the child's emotional readiness, recognizing that the soil must be fertile for the seeds of conversation to take root. The imperative lies in allowing the child ample time to return to a calm state, ensuring their emotional landscape has settled from the tumultuous waves of the meltdown into the gentle ripples of recovery. This patience allows the child to regain their sense of equilibrium, making them more receptive to dialogue. The cue often lies in the child's non-verbal signals—a relaxed posture, steady breathing, or a willingness to engage in eye contact—subtle indicators that the window for meaningful conversation has opened. It is within this space, carefully curated by patience and observance, that dialogue can unfold with the potential for healing and understanding.

I remember one time when my toddler had an epic tantrum that seemed to last forever. He was in his room, throwing everything he could get his hands on and tearing things apart. I sat there with him, feeling helpless but determined to stay present. Slowly, the storm began to wane, and his full-blown anger turned into a puddle of tears and what I can only describe as shame for his behavior. It was then that we had the most transformative talk we've ever had. My then five year old told me his emotions felt bigger than a dinosaur —like something out of a children's storybook. This led us to eventually craft a book together about these big, scary feelings. We talked about ways to tame the monster of emotions and reassured him that his mom and dad would always be there to help him navigate these scary moments. Just like we would hold his hand if there was a scary dinosaur in front of him, we are always there to hold his hand and help him navigate his scary emotions. That day, he learned he wasn't alone in his feelings, and we built a bridge of understanding that has helped us ever since.

Positive Reinforcement

The emphasis on positive reinforcement during these discussions serves as a beacon, guiding the child towards self-reflection and learning rather than entrenching them in feelings of guilt or defiance. This approach involves acknowledging the child's efforts to regain control and highlighting any strategies they employed, however imperfectly, to navigate their emotional turmoil. "I noticed you tried to use your breathing exercises when you felt upset; that's a big step." Such affirmations underscore the child's agency in managing their emotions and reinforce the value of their attempts to implement coping strategies. Positive reinforcement, woven into the fabric of post-meltdown conversations, not only nurtures the child's self-esteem but also encourages a mindset oriented towards growth and self-improvement, framing each episode not as a failure but as a stepping stone in their journey of emotional learning.

Emotional Validation

Central to these dialogues is emotional validation. This process acknowledges and accepts the child's feelings as real and significant. This validation creates a bridge of empathy, conveying to the child that their emotions, however tumultuous, are understood and respected. "It's okay to feel angry;

everyone does sometimes. What matters is how we handle that anger." Such statements validate the child's emotional experience, offering solace and understanding. This practice fosters a depth of trust between parent and child, a mutual acknowledgment that all emotions have a place in their relationship, none too dark or intense to be shared. Emotional validation, thus, becomes a cornerstone of post-meltdown conversations, laying the groundwork for open, honest dialogue that strengthens the parent-child bond and encourages emotional literacy.

In a similar manner, it can be helpful to validate your child's experience by pointing out that everyone makes mistakes. I found that once my son regained his sense of composure after huge emotional tantrums, he seems to have guilt and shame. One way that I have helped him work through this is by pointing out times I have lost my temper or acted in a way I wished I hadn't. After those moments occur I try to model acknowledging my mistakes and explaining my frustration while also apologizing for my behavior. He knows that I make mistakes, but then also sees how to handle these situations by moving forward with a better example and repairing where needed.

Learning Opportunities

Each meltdown, viewed through the lens of opportunity, becomes a classroom where lessons in emotional regulation, coping strategies, and self-awareness are imparted. These discussions, guided by a spirit of mutual learning, explore the triggers and responses associated with the meltdown, dissecting the episode to uncover insights and strategies for future encounters. "What do you think made you so upset? What could we try doing differently next time you feel that way?" Such questions posed not as inquisitions but invitations to problem-solve collaboratively, engage the child in reflective thinking. They become active participants in devising strategies for managing their emotions, empowered by the knowledge that they have a voice in their journey towards emotional regulation. This collaborative problem-solving equips the child with practical tools for managing future challenges and instills a sense of competence and resilience, qualities essential for navigating the complexities of life with ADHD.

In this nuanced healing and learning process, post-meltdown conversations emerge as pivotal moments where the groundwork for future growth is laid. Through timely engagement, positive reinforcement, emotional validation, and the collaborative exploration of learning opportunities, parents and children co-create a roadmap for navigating emotional challenges. These dialogues, rich in empathy and understanding, not only mend the rifts created by meltdowns but also forge more robust connections imbued with mutual respect and a shared commitment to growth. In the quiet aftermath of the storm lies the potential for profound transformation, a journey embarked upon together, where each step forward is guided by love, patience, and the unwavering belief in the child's capacity to learn, adapt, and thrive.

By navigating these conversations and experiences, children with ADHD embark on a journey towards self-acceptance, armed with the understanding that their unique way of interacting with the world adds invaluable depth to the human mosaic. Parents play a crucial role in facilitating discussions and creating supportive environments encouraging their children to embrace and celebrate their neurodiversity, recognizing it as a source of strength, creativity, and resilience.

I remember the first time I really engaged with my son about his ADHD. He was only seven, but he found an ADHD superhero workbook meant for older children and couldn't stop devouring it. He was so curious about what it meant for him, flipping through the pages and asking endless questions. The relief on his face as we talked was unforgettable. He seemed to light up with the realization that his ADHD was not a burden but a unique part of who he was. This experience underscored for me the importance of maintaining an open dialogue. It showed how powerful it is to create a space where children feel safe to explore and understand their neurodiversity, helping them see it as a source of strength rather than a limitation.

PREVENTING EXPLOSIVE BEHAVIOR THROUGH PREDICTIVE PLANNING

In the nuanced dance of daily life with a child with ADHD, the subtle art of predictive planning plays a pivotal role in smoothing the edges of potential upheaval. This proactive approach, far from a mere exercise in scheduling, involves a deep understanding of the child's world, an anticipatory grasp on the threads that might unravel in the face of too much stimulation, too little structure, or unexpected shifts in routine. It's a strategy that doesn't eliminate the inherent spontaneity of life but rather to buffer the impact of its less predictable moments, creating an environment where the child feels supported, understood, and, above all, capable of navigating their day with a sense of agency and calm.

Routine adjustments, while seemingly minor, can significantly influence the day-to-day experience of a child with ADHD. The key lies in recognizing that what might appear as inconsequential changes to an adult can feel monumental to a child who finds comfort in the predictability of a well-established routine. It's about observing the ebb and flow of the child's energy and attention throughout the day and aligning tasks and activities to match. A slight shift, such as moving a challenging homework assignment to a time when the child is typically more focused, or introducing a quiet, unwinding period before transitions that are historically difficult, can preempt episodes of frustration and overwhelm. These adjustments require a fluid understanding of the child's needs, a willingness to adapt, and a constant dialogue that involves the child in the process, ensuring that changes feel collaborative rather than imposed. For instance, we have to get homework done first thing when my son gets home adn has his snack. If we wait at all, my son loses his ability to focus and as the evening wanes on it becomes more and more of a battle.

Proactive communication about potential stressors stands as another pillar in the architecture of predictive planning. This dialogue, initiated well before the child encounters a stressful situation, equips them with the understanding and strategies needed to face challenges head-on. It's about creating a space where worries can be voiced and dissected, where the child's concerns are met with empathy and addressed with practical, actionable advice. Whether it's discussing the upcoming school day each morning or walking through the steps of a new social interaction, this communication builds a scaffold around the child, a framework of support that they can lean on when navigating the complexities of their day.

Environmental modifications at home and school play a crucial role in minimizing distractions and reducing sensory overload, common catalysts for explosive behavior. This might involve creating clearly defined spaces for play, study, and relaxation at home, each designed to meet the child's sensory preferences and minimize clutter and chaos. In the classroom, working with teachers to ensure the child's seating position minimizes distractions, or that there are opportunities for sensory breaks, can significantly affect the child's ability to focus and remain regulated throughout the day. These changes, tailored to the child's individual needs, transform the environment from a potential source of stress to a supportive backdrop for learning and growth.

Anticipatory guidance, the practice of teaching children to foresee and plan for situations that might be challenging, empowers them with a sense of preparedness and control. This skill development involves role-playing, where hypothetical scenarios are explored, and the child is guided in identifying potential responses. It also includes using social stories that illustrate everyday social interactions or changes in routine, providing a blueprint for the child to follow. By equipping the child with the tools to anticipate and strategize, parents and caregivers foster a sense of competence and self-efficacy, reducing the child's reliance on immediate emotional responses and encouraging a more reflective, considered approach to navigating their world.

By navigating these conversations and experiences, children with ADHD embark on a journey towards self-acceptance, armed with the understanding that their unique way of interacting with the world adds invaluable depth to the human mosaic. Parents play a crucial role in facilitating discussions and creating supportive environments encouraging their children to embrace and celebrate their neurodiversity, recognizing it as a source of strength, creativity, and resilience.

I remember the first time I really engaged with my son about his ADHD. He was only seven, but he found an ADHD superhero workbook I had bought but then realized it was meant for older children and I hid it, but after he found it he couldn't stop devouring it. He wanted to know what the letters stood for and what they meant. He was so curious about what it meant for him, flipping through the pages and asking endless questions. The relief on his face as we talked was unforgettable. He seemed to light up with the realization that his ADHD was not a burden but a unique part of who he was. This experience underscored for me the importance of maintaining an open dialogue. It showed how powerful it is to create a space where children feel safe to explore and understand their neurodiversity, helping them see it as a source of strength rather than a limitation.

This proactive, predictive approach to planning doesn't just mitigate the potential for explosive behavior; it builds a foundation from which the child can confidently explore their world, armed with the knowledge that they possess the tools and strategies to face whatever comes their way. It's a journey toward minimizing challenging behavior and empowering the child with ADHD to navigate their day-today life with a greater sense of autonomy, resilience, and self-knowing.

In reflecting on the strategies discussed, the broader picture emerges of empowerment and proactive engagement. We've traversed the landscape of predictive planning, exploring how slight adjustments in routine, open lines of communication, thoughtful changes in the environment, and the teaching of anticipatory skills can significantly impact a child with ADHD's ability to navigate their world. These strategies, rooted in understanding the child's unique needs and fostering a sense of agency, set the stage for a life where challenges are met with confidence and resilience. As we move forward, these principles of proactive planning and empowerment will continue to guide us, offering a beacon of hope and a pathway to growth for children with ADHD and their families.

YOUR THOUGHTS MATTER
(AND CAN HELP SOMEONE LIKE YOU!)

A Small Favor That Goes a Long Way

"When we understand the neurodivergent mind, we don't just parent; we empower. If this book has guided you toward new breakthroughs, your review could be the lifeline another parent is searching for."

MEGAN HILL, PHD

Hey there! If you're enjoying this book so far (or even if you're just muddling through like the rest of us!), I'd love to ask you for a quick favor. Sharing your thoughts can actually help a ton of other parents who are on the same rollercoaster ride.

Think about when you were hunting for a book that would really "get" your situation—reviews probably made a difference, right? Your words could be the nudge someone needs to dive in and feel less alone, more hopeful, and better equipped to tackle the chaos.

I know leaving a review isn't always top of mind (trust me, I get it—life is busy!), but it takes just a minute and could mean the world to another parent in the trenches. Here's what your review might do:

- Help a mom who's drowning in overwhelm find some much-needed guidance.

- Give a dad searching for practical tips a little hope and a lot of new ideas.
- Remind a fellow parent that, yes, someone else is dealing with this too—and thriving through it.

If you've found even a nugget of something helpful in these pages, I'd be so grateful if you'd share it. Just scan the QR code or hit the link below to leave a review:

Leave Review Here

Thanks for being here with me on this wild journey. Your voice really does matter!

All the best,

Megan Hill, PhD

CHAPTER 6
STEERING THROUGH EMOTIONAL SKIES: SELF-REGULATION IN CHILDREN WITH ADHD

Imagine a leaf tumbling through the air, its path dictated by the whims of the wind. At times, it soars; at others, it spirals unpredictably. This leaf, caught in the gusts of its journey, mirrors the emotional world of a child with ADHD—full of highs and lows, sudden turns, and unexpected pauses. The quest for balance, for a steady course amidst these emotional eddies, brings us to the doorstep of self-regulation—a skill not innate but cultivated, crucial for navigating not just childhood but the entirety of life's unpredictable weather.

SELF-REGULATION SKILLS FOR DIFFERENT AGES AND STAGES

Developmental Considerations

Self-regulation evolves, and its facets change as a child grows. For toddlers, it might mean mastering the impulse to grab toys from peers. School-aged children learn to sit through lessons, attention tethered to the teacher's words. Teenagers face the complex dance of managing academic pressures alongside burgeoning social lives. Each stage demands strategies that resonate with the child's cognitive and emotional capacity. Recognizing these developmental milestones informs the tailoring of self-regulation strategies, ensuring they align with the child's evolving abilities.

Visual Schedules

In a world that often feels chaotic, visual schedules serve as anchors, offering a tangible representation of the day's structure. For a child struggling to grasp the abstract concept of time, a visual schedule transforms the day's expectations into a series of manageable, sequential steps. It might depict icons for school, homework, play, and bedtime, each accompanied by a clock showing the start time. This tool not only aids in understanding and managing daily tasks but also reduces anxiety about transitions, providing a clear roadmap for the day ahead.

Reward Systems

Motivation waxes and wanes, its fires needing stoking, especially in children for whom immediate rewards speak louder than distant promises. Implementing a reward system then becomes a dialogue in motivation and a way to incentivize the practice of self-regulation skills. Consider a sticker chart for younger children, where stickers lead to a cherished reward—a trip to the park or an extra bedtime story. For older children, a points system might translate into privileges, like screen time or outings with friends. These systems, grounded in the principles of positive reinforcement, highlight progress, making the intangible tangible.

Role-Playing

The social world is a stage, and its dynamics are often puzzling to children with ADHD. Parents and educators can rehearse social scenarios with the child through role-playing, from sharing toys to navigating disagreements. A safe and structured rehearsal space allows the child to explore different responses and consider the why behind actions and reactions. It's in the act of stepping into another's shoes that empathy is fostered, and self-regulation strategies are internalized, preparing the child for the multifaceted social interactions that await them beyond the home and classroom.

Another powerful use of role-playing is in preparing for potential disagreements or conflicts. Suppose your child often has difficulty staying calm when things don't go their way. You can create a scenario where something unexpected happens, like a game not going according to plan, and guide your child through expressing their feelings calmly and finding a solution together. By discussing the "why" behind each reaction during the role-play, you help your child understand the impact of their actions on others and on themselves.

This practice not only helps children develop empathy by seeing situations from different perspectives but also equips them with self-regulation strategies that can be drawn upon in real-life social interactions. Role-playing thus becomes a valuable rehearsal for the multifaceted social world, building your child's confidence and ability to handle various social dynamics with grace and understanding.

Strategy Section: Creating a Self-Regulation Toolkit for Families

Developing self-regulation skills is crucial for children with ADHD as they navigate the complexities of their emotions and impulses. A Self-Regulation Toolkit can be an invaluable resource for families, offering practical tools and strategies to help children build these essential skills in a supportive and engaging way. Here's how to create your own self-regulation toolkit:

1. Customizable Visual Schedules

- Purpose: Visual schedules help children understand and manage their time by providing a clear structure for their day.
- How to Create: Use templates to create daily or weekly schedules that can be customized to fit your family's routine. Include time slots for activities such as meals, homework, playtime, and bedtime.
- Tips: Incorporate visual cues like pictures or icons for younger children who may not yet read. Allow your child to help create and update the schedule to increase their engagement and sense of ownership.

2. Reward Systems

- Purpose: Reward systems motivate children to develop positive behaviors and self-regulation skills by reinforcing desired actions.
- How to Create: Design a reward chart that tracks progress toward specific goals, such as completing tasks on time or managing emotions during stressful situations. Printable stickers and charts can be used to make the system more engaging.
- Tips: Tailor the rewards to your child's age and interests. For younger children, small rewards like extra playtime or a special treat might be motivating. For older children, consider rewards that align with their hobbies or interests, like earning time for a favorite activity.

3. Role-Playing Scenarios

- Purpose: Role-playing allows children to practice social interactions and emotional responses in a safe environment.
- How to Create: Develop scenarios that reflect common challenges your child may face, such as sharing toys, handling disappointment, or resolving conflicts. Provide dialogue prompts and reflection questions to guide the role-play.
- Tips: Act out these scenarios with your child, taking turns in different roles. After the role-play, discuss what worked well and what could be improved. This helps your child internalize the lessons and apply them in real-life situations.

4. Sensory Tools

- Purpose: Sensory tools help children manage overwhelming emotions by providing a physical outlet for stress.
- How to Create: Include items such as stress balls, fidget toys, or even a "calm-down" jar filled with glitter and water. These tools can be used during moments of high stress to help your child regain focus and calm down.
- Tips: Keep these sensory tools in a designated "calm corner" where your child can go when they need to self-regulate. Teach them how to use these tools during calm moments so they can effectively use them when emotions run high.

5. Breathing Exercises

- Purpose: Breathing exercises help regulate the nervous system and bring a sense of calm during stressful moments.
- How to Create: Teach your child simple breathing techniques such as "balloon breathing," where they imagine inflating a balloon with their belly as they inhale and slowly deflate it as they exhale. Another technique is "square breathing," where they trace a square in the air, inhaling and holding their breath as they trace each side.
- Tips: Practice these exercises regularly, not just in stressful moments but also as a part of the daily routine. This will help your child become more familiar with the techniques and more likely to use

them when needed.

Implementation and Consistency

Once your Self-Regulation Toolkit is assembled, the key to its effectiveness is consistency. Regularly use the tools and strategies in the toolkit as part of your child's daily routine. Encourage your child to participate in using and updating the toolkit, making it a dynamic and evolving resource that grows with your child's needs.

By creating and implementing a Self-Regulation Toolkit, families can build a structured yet flexible system that supports the development of self-regulation skills in children with ADHD. This toolkit not only equips children with practical strategies to manage their emotions and behaviors but also fosters a sense of empowerment and confidence as they learn to navigate their world with greater skill and resilience.

In the fabric of everyday life, woven with threads of challenge and triumph, the development of self-regulation skills emerges as a pivotal element in the tapestry of childhood, especially for those navigating the complexities of ADHD. Through the thoughtful application of strategies tailored to the child's developmental stage, the use of visual schedules to demystify the abstract nature of time, the motivation woven through reward systems, and the empathetic understanding fostered by role-playing, children with ADHD are equipped not just to face the gusts of emotion and impulse but to navigate them with skill and confidence. This chapter, dedicated to the art and science of cultivating self-regulation, offers strategies and a lens to view the emotional development of children with ADHD—a perspective that sees potential, resilience, and the capacity for growth in every tumble and soar of the journey.

MINDFULNESS AND MEDITATION TECHNIQUES FOR FOCUS

Within the kaleidoscope of strategies aimed at nurturing focus and equilibrium in children with ADHD, mindfulness, and meditation emerge not as mere ancillary practices but as foundational elements. Their potency lies in the gentle recalibration of attention, the subtle realignment of the mind's compass towards the present moment—a skill of immeasurable value for those whose thoughts often race ahead or lag behind in the stream of consciousness.

Introduction to Mindfulness

At its core, mindfulness constitutes an awareness, an acute consciousness of the here and now, experienced without judgment or distraction. For a child whose world is a whirlwind of stimuli, where focus flits like a butterfly from one interest to another, mindfulness offers a pause, a breath in constant motion. It is the act of noticing—the texture of a leaf, the coolness of the air, the myriad of sounds that fill a room—each observation a tether to the present. The benefits for children with ADHD are manifold, from enhanced concentration and emotional regulation to a reduction in impulsivity, each a stepping stone towards a more centered and peaceful state of being.

Simple Meditation Practices

Introducing children to meditation begins with simplicity, with practices distilled to their essence, accessible and engaging for young minds. One such practice is the "Mindful Minute," a challenge wrapped in an adventure, where the child is invited to sit quietly, eyes closed, and listen to the sounds around them for one full minute. The goal is not silence but attention, to anchor their thoughts to the act of listening, noticing the layers of sound that unfold. Another practice involves visualization, guiding the child to imagine a place of great happiness and peace, exploring this space in their mind's eye, each detail a brushstroke in their portrait of tranquility. These practices, brief yet potent, serve as introductions to the broader world of meditation, each session a building block in cultivating mindfulness.

Breathing for Focus

Breathing, the most fundamental of acts, holds within its rhythm the capacity to center and stabilize. For children with ADHD, learning to harness their breath as a tool for focus is transformative. The practice of "Square Breathing" illustrates this beautifully—a visual and tactile exercise, discussed in the previous chapter, where the child breathes in for a count of four, holds for four, exhales for four, and holds again for four, tracing a square in the air with their finger as they do so. This systematic process, where breathing becomes a physical and mental exercise, draws the child's attention inward, quieting the noise of distraction and sharpening their focus like a lens coming into clear resolution. It is a skill that, once learned, becomes a refuge, a haven they can return to time and again when the world becomes too loud, too fast, too much.

Mindful Moments

Integrating mindful moments into the daily fabric of a child's life embeds the principles of mindfulness into their routine, making it as natural a practice as brushing their teeth or tying their shoes. These moments can be as structured as beginning each day with a minute of mindful breathing before school or as spontaneous as taking a "mindful walk," where each step is taken with intention. The surroundings are observed with fresh eyes. Another technique involves using a "mindfulness bell" app that chimes at random intervals throughout the day; each chimes a prompt for the child to pause, take a deep breath, and name one thing they can see, hear, and feel in that moment. These practices, woven into the child's day, encourage a habitual return to the present, fostering an environment where impulsivity is tempered by reflection, where the mind, so often scattered, finds its anchor in the now.

In this exploration of mindfulness and meditation as tools for focus and self-regulation, we uncover not just strategies but a philosophy—a way of engaging with the world that honors each moment, each breath as worthy of attention. For children with ADHD, these practices open doors to new ways of experiencing their thoughts, their emotions, and their interactions with the world around them. They learn that focus is not a finite resource, depleted and scattered, but a wellspring that, with mindfulness, can be tapped, deepened, and enriched. Through the introduction of simple meditation practices, the strategic use of breathing for focus, and the seamless integration of mindful moments into daily life, we offer these children a gift—a set of keys to unlock a world where the present is not a blur passed in haste but a space of clarity, calm, and profound engagement.

USING PLAY TO ENHANCE SELF-CONTROL AND ATTENTION

Structured play, often mistaken for formal learning experiences, is actually a vibrant mosaic of activities carefully crafted to enhance focus and self-discipline in children, especially those managing the challenges of ADHD. This form of play, far from the rigidity its name might suggest, thrives on creativity, weaving together elements of fun and engagement with the subtle threads of learning objectives. Picture, for instance, a game of 'Simon Says,' where children must filter commands through attentive listening, acting only when the phrase is preceded by the magic words "Simon says." This simple game, a staple of childhood play, doubles as a crucible for developing impulse control and attentive listening, skills critical for children with ADHD. Each round, filled with laughter and movement, becomes a dynamic arena where following directions and sharpening focus occur not as chores but as delightful challenges to be met with eagerness.

Transitioning to the embrace of the outdoors, activities beneath the vast expanse of the sky offer a change of scenery and a profound shift in how children with ADHD engage with the world around them. With its inherent unpredictability and sensory richness, outdoor play presents a natural setting for cultivating attention and reducing hyperactivity. Consider the act of building a fort from branches and leaves in a wooded area; this task, requiring planning, persistence, and problem-solving, anchors the child's attention to a tangible goal, their focus undivided as they navigate the intricacies of construction. Meanwhile, the sensory input from the natural environment—the texture of the bark, the rustle of leaves, the dappling of sunlight through the canopy—grounds the child in the present, their usually scattered attention honed in on the task at hand. Outdoor activities, from hiking on a forest trail to the rhythmic repetition of jumping rope, merge physical exertion with sensory engagement, creating a potent mix that fosters concentration while simultaneously siphoning off excess energy.

A discerning eye can identify those that strike a harmonious balance between challenge and enjoyment by delving into games and toys designed to enhance concentration and patience. Board games that require strategic thinking and planning, such as chess or checkers, invite players into a mental dance of anticipation and decision-making. Each move, contemplated with care, becomes a lesson in patience and foresight, the child's attention riveted to the evolving patterns on the board. Puzzle-based toys, including jigsaw puzzles and intricate building sets, operate on a similar frequency, demanding sustained concentration as the child navigates the path from chaos to cohesion, piece by piece. These games, selected not merely for their entertainment value but for their capacity to build cognitive skills, transform playtime into a fertile ground for developing focus and self-control.

The expressive power of the creative arts—art, music, and dance—serves as a multifaceted tool for children with ADHD, offering outlets for emotion, windows for focus, and platforms for expression. With their endless spectrum of colors, shapes, and textures, visual arts invite children into a world where focus is drawn tightly to the tip of a brush, the stroke of a pencil, or the melding of hues on a palette. This immersion in the creative process provides a quiet center in the storm of distractions, the act of creation of a meditative practice that harnesses the child's scattered attention and channels it into the manifestation of their vision. Music, with its rhythms and melodies, acts as both an anchor and a sail, grounding the child in the rhythm of the moment while allowing their emotions and thoughts to voyage through the notes. Learning an instrument, for instance, melds cognitive engagement with emotional expression, and each note plays a victory in the battle for focus and self-discipline. Dance, the most kinetic of the arts, marries movement with mindfulness, the child's body becoming an instrument of their attention as they navigate the choreography of steps and sequences. The discipline required to master movements to synchronize body and mind to the music cultivates a level of attention and control that transcends the dance studio, rippling outward into all areas of the child's life.

In this exploration of play as a vehicle for enhancing self-control and attention in children with ADHD, a landscape rich with opportunity and variety emerges. From the structured challenges of 'Simon Says' to the immersive engagement of the arts, each activity, carefully chosen and mindfully engaged in, becomes a brick in the foundation of focus and self-discipline. This approach to play, recognizing its potential as both a learning tool and a source of joy, offers children with ADHD a path to harness their vibrant energies and expansive imaginations, not as obstacles to be overcome but as strengths to be celebrated and directed towards the achievement of their fullest potential.

TAILORING EDUCATIONAL CONTENT TO MAINTAIN FOCUS

In the intricate landscape of educational strategies for children with ADHD, adapting content to sustain focus goes beyond traditional teaching methods, evolving into a dynamic blend of interests, hands-on learning, sensory experiences, and digital tools. Far from merely adapting content, this approach represents a holistic reimagining of the learning experience designed to captivate, engage, and inspire young minds prone to distraction.

Interest-based learning emerges not as a novel concept but as a pivotal strategy in captivating the attention of children with ADHD, transforming the educational landscape into a realm where curiosity leads, and learning follows. This method, rooted in the child's passions—dinosaurs, the cosmos, or the intricate mechanics of machines—becomes a lens through which traditional subjects are explored, ensuring engagement is not a fleeting visitor but a constant companion in the child's educational journey. By weaving these interests into the fabric of subjects from math to literature, educators, and parents craft a curriculum that speaks directly to the child's heart, ensuring that focus is captured not by the effort of will but by the allure of genuine fascination.

The rhythm of learning for a child with ADHD benefits significantly from incorporating breaks and movement, acknowledging that the body's need to move can be a powerful ally in the quest for sustained concentration. These breaks, strategically placed like intermissions in the learning flow, provide respite and rejuvenation, allowing the child to return to the task at hand with renewed vigor. Movement activities, from simple stretches to brief, heart-raising exercises, act as reset buttons for the mind, dissipating restlessness and sharpening focus. When integrated into the learning process, this kinetic interlude ensures that the child's natural movement becomes a bridge to better attention rather than a barrier.

In acknowledging the multifaceted nature of focus for children with ADHD, multi-sensory learning methods stand out as critical tools in engaging a variety of sensory pathways, thereby enhancing understanding and retention. This approach, which might involve the tactile exploration of materials during a science lesson or the auditory stimulation of listening to a story while following along in the book, caters to the diverse ways children with ADHD absorb and process information. By engaging multiple senses, educators and caregivers create a rich array of stimuli that holds the child's attention, making learning an immersive experience that transcends the passive receipt of information, transforming it into an active, multi-dimensional exploration.

Integrating technology aids and apps to support focus and learning represents a confluence of innovation and education, offering tools specifically designed to meet the unique needs of children with ADHD. From applications that break tasks into manageable segments to programs that use gamification to teach math, reading, or coding skills, technology becomes a tailor-made companion in the educational journey of a child with ADHD. These digital tools, carefully selected to align with the child's interests and learning objectives, sustain attention and offer immediate feedback and a sense of accomplishment, critical drivers in maintaining motivation and engagement.

In orchestrating educational content tailored to the unique rhythms and requirements of children with ADHD, a symphony of strategies emerges—each note, from interest-based learning to the incorporation of technology, plays its part in maintaining focus and fostering a love for learning. This approach, rich in adaptability and innovation, acknowledges the child's individuality, crafting an educational experience that is as engaging as it is enlightening.

As we close this exploration of tailored educational strategies, we find ourselves not at an end but at a threshold, poised on the brink of further discovery. The insights garnered here—spanning the realms of personal interests, kinetic learning, sensory engagement, and digital tools—offer not just methods but a mindset, a way of envisioning education as diverse and dynamic as the children it seeks to inspire. In this reimagined learning landscape, every child finds their place, their path illuminated by strategies that speak to their unique strengths and challenges. This chapter, then, is but a single step in a broader journey towards understanding and empowering children with ADHD, a journey that continues to unfold with each page turned, each strategy implemented, and each child's potential unlocked.

CHAPTER 7
CULTIVATING EMOTIONAL INTELLIGENCE IN ADHD

Amidst the hustle of daily routines, the rush of deadlines, and the endless stream of responsibilities, the emotional world of a child with ADHD can often feel chaotic and overwhelming, yet full of potential. I've seen this firsthand with my own child, who can be a whirlwind of emotions, both challenging and beautiful. This emotional complexity is crucial for building deep connections, understanding, and growth. By carefully nurturing their emotional development—through patience, open conversations, and support—we can help them develop resilience, empathy, and self-awareness. It's in these everyday moments of care and attention that we lay the groundwork for their emotional growth and well-being.

EMOTIONAL LITERACY: TEACHING KIDS TO NAME THEIR FEELINGS

Feeling Vocabulary

A child's emotional vocabulary is the palette from which they paint their experiences, feelings, and needs. Expanding this palette goes beyond mere word acquisition; it's an invitation to explore the nuances of their inner landscape, to recognize and name the hues of joy, frustration, sadness, and excitement that color their world. Similar to how an artist learns to differentiate between cerulean and azure, a child, guided by thoughtful conversation and attentive listening, learns to distinguish between anger and disappointment, happiness and contentment. This discernment is crucial not only for the child's self-expression but also for their understanding of others. It's in the quiet moments, perhaps during a shared afternoon walk, when a parent might point to the sky, noting not just its blueness but the soft blend of colors at dusk, drawing a parallel to the complex mix of feelings a child might experience at the end of a school day.

I remember one evening when my son came home from school visibly upset. We sat on the porch together, watching the sunset, and I gently asked him to describe how she was feeling. He struggled at first, but with a bit of encouragement, he began to talk about his day, naming his emotions one by one—frustration over a difficult math test, sadness from a misunderstanding with a friend, and a touch of happiness from art class. As we talked, I helped him see how each feeling was valid and how they all blended together, much like the colors in the sky. This moment not only helped him process his emotions but also deepened our connection, showing him that he could always come to me to untangle his feelings and find clarity.

Emotion Charts

Visual aids, such as emotion charts or wheels, serve as tangible guides in the child's exploration of their feelings. Positioned within easy reach, perhaps on the refrigerator door or beside the child's study area, these charts offer a visual vocabulary, a map to navigate the often tumultuous terrain of emotions. Each glance pointing to a face or word that resonates with their current state strengthens the child's ability to identify and articulate feelings. This simple yet profound tool not only aids in immediate emotional identification but also fosters a habit of reflection and self-awareness, laying the groundwork for more complex emotional understanding as they grow.

We first introduced emotion charts during kindergarten with our son, and they quickly became an essential part of our household. I remember the day he brought one home from school, excited to show us how he could use it to describe his feelings. Placing the chart on our refrigerator, it became a go-to reference during our daily conversations. Whenever he felt overwhelmed or unsure of his emotions, he would point to the chart, finding the face or word that matched his feelings. This practice made discussing emotions a regular part of our routine, helping him—and us —navigate the ups and downs of each day with greater clarity and empathy. Over time, these charts not only helped him articulate his emotions but also opened up deeper discussions about why he felt a certain way and how we could support each other through it.

Reading Emotions

The art of reading emotions in oneself and others is like learning to decipher a complex language without words, a language of facial expressions, tone of voice, and body language. I remember one evening when we decided to watch a muted scene from our favorite family movie. We took turns guessing the characters' feelings based solely on their non-verbal cues. It was a fun and enlightening exercise, and my son got really into it, laughing and concentrating as he tried to read the characters' emotions. This activity emphasized the importance of paying close attention, encouraging him to look beyond the surface and truly empathize with others. Over time, this skill has enriched his interactions and relationships, allowing him to connect more deeply and understand the emotions behind the gestures and expressions he encounters every day

Expressing Needs

Constructively expressing one's emotional needs is a cornerstone of emotional intelligence. For a child with ADHD, whose emotions might often feel overwhelming or confusing, learning to communicate these needs clearly and healthily is empowering. I remember one afternoon when my son seemed particularly frustrated but couldn't quite articulate why. We decided to role-play different scenarios where he could practice asking for space, time, or help. Through these playful yet meaningful exercises, he began to feel more comfortable expressing his needs. Over time, we reinforced this practice in our daily interactions by actively listening and responding to what he communicated. This validation not only helped him feel understood but also showed him that expressing his needs is a natural and important part of relationships. It taught him that sharing his feelings is not a burden but a form of self-respect and consideration for those around him.

Strategy Section: Creating and Implementing an Interactive Emotion Wheel

Helping children with ADHD navigate their emotions can be a crucial part of fostering emotional intelligence and building stronger family connections. An Interactive Emotion Wheel is an engaging and hands-on tool that can be used to encourage children to explore and express their feelings in a structured and supportive way. Below is a step-by-step guide on how to create and implement an Interactive Emotion Wheel in your home.

Creating the Interactive Emotion Wheel

1. Gather Materials:

- A sturdy base for the wheel, such as a cardboard circle or a wooden disc.
- A spinner (you can make one with an arrow cutout and a brad or use a pre-made spinner).
- Markers or paints to decorate the wheel.
- Stickers, images, or drawings of facial expressions representing various emotions.

- Labels for emotions (e.g., happy, sad, angry, excited, frustrated, calm, etc.).

2. Design the Wheel:

- Divide the wheel into sections, with each section representing a different emotion.
- In each section, place a corresponding facial expression that visually represents that emotion.
- Label each section with the appropriate emotion word.
- Decorate the wheel in a way that is engaging for your child—bright colors, favorite characters, or themes that resonate with them can make the wheel more appealing.

3. Customize It:

- Involve your child in the creation process by letting them choose some of the emotions or help with the decoration. This personalization helps them feel more connected to the tool and more likely to use it regularly.

Implementing the Emotion Wheel in Your Home

1. Establish a Routine:

- Use the wheel as a daily check-in tool, either in the morning to start the day or in the evening to reflect on the day's experiences.

- Make spinning the wheel a part of your child's routine, so it becomes a natural and expected activity.

2. Use It as a Conversation Starter:

- Once your child lands on an emotion, ask open-ended questions like, "What happened today that made you feel this way?" or "Can you tell me more about why you're feeling [emotion]?"
- Encourage your child to talk about specific events or triggers that led to that emotion, helping them make connections between their feelings and experiences.

3. Discuss Coping Strategies:

- Depending on the emotion, guide your child in exploring different coping strategies. For example, if they land on "angry," discuss deep breathing exercises, taking a break, or talking through the frustration.
- Use the wheel to brainstorm together what might help them feel better or manage the emotion more effectively.

4. Reinforce Emotional Literacy:

- Over time, the regular use of the Emotion Wheel helps your child build a vocabulary for their feelings, making it easier for them to express themselves in various situations.

- Encourage your child to use the wheel independently when they feel overwhelmed, helping them recognize and manage their emotions on their own.

5. Strengthen Family Connections:

- Make the Emotion Wheel a shared family activity by having everyone in the family take turns using it. This fosters an environment where emotions are openly discussed and understood.
- Celebrate the progress your child makes in identifying and expressing their emotions, reinforcing the positive impact of this tool.

The Interactive Emotion Wheel is more than just a tool; it's a gateway to deeper emotional understanding and connection within your family. By integrating this simple yet powerful resource into your daily routine, you help your child develop essential emotional literacy skills while creating a space where feelings are recognized, discussed, and supported.

In nurturing the garden of a child's emotional world, we cultivate a landscape where feelings are recognized, named, and expressed with confidence and clarity. Through the expansion of emotional vocabulary, the use of visual aids like emotion charts, activities that enhance the reading of emotions, and the encouragement of healthy emotional expression, we lay the foundation for a rich emotional life. This foundation, built on understanding and empathy, supports not just the child's interpersonal relationships but also their relationship with themselves, fostering a deep, abiding emotional intelligence that guides them through the complexities of life with ADHD.

STRATEGIES FOR DEVELOPING EMOTIONAL REGULATION

In the quiet spaces between the chaos of daily life, where silence speaks volumes and breaths are measured in moments of calm, lies the fertile ground for nurturing emotional regulation in children with ADHD. I've found that these moments often come unexpectedly, like when we're cuddled up with a book before bedtime or taking a leisurely walk in the park. It's in these times that we can deliberately pause and shift towards practices that ground and guide. Instead of constantly directing and overseeing, I've learned to collaborate with my child, discovering together what strategies work best for managing the waves of emotion. We experiment, practice, and refine these techniques, creating a shared journey towards greater emotional stability and understanding.

Modeling Regulation

The act of modeling emotional regulation, for a parent, is akin to setting the sails on a ship, demonstrating how to catch the wind in just the right way to navigate smoothly. A child learns the art of emotional steadiness through the observation of calm, considered responses to frustration or disappointment. Consider the scenario where a parent, faced with an unexpected change in plans that derails the day's schedule, takes a deep breath, their demeanor reflective of disappointment yet underpinned by a visible resilience. They articulate their feelings, acknowledging the upset while highlighting their thought process toward finding a solution or accepting the situation. This behavior, observed by the child, becomes a blueprint for managing their responses to similar situations. It is not merely the words spoken but the actions taken—the deep breaths, the calm articulation of feelings, the visible processing of emotion—that serve as the most potent lessons in emotional regulation.

One day, the wheels were metaphorically falling off the bus at our house. The laundry was piling up, dinner was burning, and the kids were all over the place. I lost my temper for a moment, but then I decided to exaggerate a bit. I plopped down in the middle of the chaos, crossed my legs, closed my eyes, and started humming loudly as if I were meditating. My toddler found this absolutely hilarious, but what surprised me most was seeing him mimic this behavior in the following days. Whenever he got frustrated, he'd plop down, cross his little legs, and hum loudly just like I did. It was a funny and endearing reminder that our kids really do watch and learn from everything we do, sometimes even taking our silliest actions to heart.

Coping Mechanisms

Introducing and practicing coping mechanisms with children acts as the keel that keeps the ship steady in stormy seas. These varied and personalized mechanisms range from tactile strategies, like squeezing a stress ball, to cognitive ones, such as envisioning a peaceful place. A favorite activity in our house is belly breathing exercises. We pretend there's a balloon in our bellies that we slowly fill up with air. The key lies in exploring and identifying strategies that resonate with the child, followed by regular practice. A routine might be established where, at the first hint of frustration or anger, the child is encouraged to choose a coping mechanism, perhaps visualizing themselves in their 'happy place'—a beach, a forest, or even a cozy corner of their home. This practice, repeated over time, strengthens the child's ability to summon calm at will, turning what might once have been an automatic reaction into a choice, a moment of pause where they can select how to respond.

Emotion-Coaching

Emotion-coaching transforms a parent from a mere observer to an active participant in their child's emotional development. This technique involves validating the child's feelings, helping them to name what they are experiencing, and guiding them toward understanding why they might feel a certain way. It's a dialogue that unfolds in layers, where initial acknowledgment of the emotion—"I can see you're feeling really upset"—is followed by gentle probing that encourages the child to reflect on the source of their feelings and consider alternative responses. Through emotion coaching, children learn to identify and understand their emotions and see their feelings as signals and information that can guide their reactions and decisions. It's a nuanced approach that builds emotional intelligence, equipping the child with the tools to navigate their inner world with insight and empathy.

Stress Management

Teaching children stress management techniques tailored to their comprehension and capacity involves guiding them through new and unfamiliar experiences. Simple yet effective techniques provide children with anchors of calm amid stress. Breathing exercises designed to slow the heart rate and bring awareness to the present moment can be introduced through games that engage the practice, like blowing bubbles to see who can make the largest one with a long, slow breath out. Progressive muscle relaxation, another technique, can be taught through storytelling, where the child tenses and relaxes different muscle groups along with the characters in the story. For older children, mindfulness activities that promote focused attention, such as mindful eating or walking, can be integrated into daily routines, offering moments of peace and presence. When woven into the fabric of daily life, these practices provide immediate relief from stress and build a foundation of skills that the child can draw upon throughout their life.

In navigating the intricate dance of developing emotional regulation in children with ADHD, caregivers embark on a journey that is both challenging and deeply rewarding. Through modeling regulation, introducing and refining coping mechanisms, engaging in emotion-coaching, and teaching stress management techniques, they lay down stepping stones for the child to cross from the realms of impulse and reaction into those of reflection and choice. This path, marked by patience, practice, and persistence, leads towards a horizon where emotional regulation becomes not just a skill learned but a natural part of the child's approach to life, a testament to the transformative power of careful, compassionate guidance in the growth journey.

Despite how simple it may sound, this process was quite difficult in our house. Teaching and reinforcing these skills required consistent effort and patience. There were countless moments during tantrums and overwhelming days when I wanted to pull my hair out or hide in the bathroom for a bit of peace. But in those moments, I would try my hardest to take a deep breath, remind myself that this was all part of the journey, and try to model the calm I hoped to see. Over time, we really have seen improvement. With each small step forward, we've watched our child grow more capable of managing emotions. These little victories remind us that persistence truly pays off in fostering emotional resilience, even if it means surviving a few chaotic moments along the way.

And, I think it is really important to say that it's okay that we aren't perfect. There have been times when I've flown off the handle, lost my patience, or reacted in ways I wish I hadn't. But instead of dwelling on those moments, I've learned to use them as valuable teaching opportunities. I talk to my kids about what happened, openly acknowledging my mistakes and discussing how I could have handled things better. I might say, "You know, when I got really frustrated earlier, I didn't take the deep breaths I should have. Next time, I'll try to remember to pause before I react." This not only shows them that everyone messes up sometimes, but it also reinforces the importance of accountability and growth. It teaches them that making mistakes is a natural part of life, and what really matters is how we learn from those mistakes and strive to do better next time. By modeling this mindset, we create a family environment where vulnerability is accepted, growth is celebrated, and everyone—adults and children alike—feels supported in their journey to become their best selves.

BUILDING RESILIENCE THROUGH PROBLEM-SOLVING SKILLS

In the complex process of a child's development, the ability to navigate daily challenges with agility and insight reflects their growing resilience. Developing problem-solving skills is like strengthening a muscle; it requires nurturing through deliberate practice, guided exploration, and supportive feedback. For children, especially those with ADHD, this journey is filled with opportunities hidden within obstacles. Each challenge presents a lesson in disguise, offering a chance for them to stretch their wings and test their resolve.

Problem-Solving Steps

The initiation into problem-solving begins with distilling a seemingly formidable task into a series of simple, manageable steps. This process, akin to laying out the pieces of a puzzle before attempting to piece them together, involves identifying the problem, brainstorming possible solutions, evaluating these options, choosing a course of action, and finally, reflecting on the outcome. For a child, this breakdown transforms the overwhelming into the achievable. It's a systematic approach that demystifies the process, turning the abstract concept of 'problem-solving' into a concrete sequence of actions. Parents and educators can facilitate this learning by posing hypothetical scenarios drawn from the pages of the child's favorite stories or inspired by real-life situations and guiding the child through each step. Repeated over time, this exercise ingrains a problem-solving template in the child's cognitive toolkit, a scaffold upon which they can construct their strategies as they encounter challenges.

Role-Playing Scenarios

Role-playing emerges as a dynamic stage upon which children can rehearse the art of problem-solving within the safety of a controlled environment. This method, breathing life into hypothetical scenarios, allows children to step into roles, navigate conflicts, and explore resolutions in real time. Imagine a scenario where two characters must share a coveted toy, a situation ripe with potential conflict and negotiation. Through role-play, children can experiment with various solutions, weighing the outcomes of sharing versus competing and collaboration against confrontation. This immersive experience enhances their problem-solving abilities and cultivates empathy as they view the world through another's eyes, understanding motivations and emotions different from theirs. The controlled setting provides a safety net, a place where mistakes are:

- Learning opportunities.
- Not grounds for reprimand.
- Encouraging children to take risks and experiment with solutions.

Overcoming Obstacles

Framing obstacles as opportunities rather than impediments plays a crucial role in fostering resilience. This subtle, profound perspective shift encourages a mindset that leans into challenges, viewing them as puzzles to be solved and mysteries to be unraveled. For a child with ADHD, who might face more than their fair share of hurdles, this reframe is empowering. It instills a sense of agency, an understanding that they hold the keys to overcoming the barriers before them. This empowerment is nurtured through dialogue and reflection, where each challenge encountered is dissected to uncover the learning within. Parents can facilitate this shift through language emphasizing growth and potential, celebrating the effort and strategy over the outcome. It's a conversation highlighting the silver linings, the unexpected skills honed, and the knowledge gained in the face of adversity, weaving a narrative where resilience is the hero, emerging stronger with each obstacle navigated.

Supportive Feedback

The role of feedback, when dispensed with care and consideration, cannot be overstated in its importance to the development of problem-solving skills and resilience. This feedback, however, diverges from the traditional notions of critique, embracing instead a form that is constructive, specific, and imbued with positive reinforcement. It's feedback that acknowledges the effort and the thought process behind the decision-making, even if the outcome wasn't as intended. This acknowledgment acts as a beacon for children, guiding their journey through the murky waters of problem-solving and reassuring them that their efforts are seen, valued, and appreciated. It's a delicate balance, offering guidance that nudges them towards reflecting and refining their strategies without diminishing their sense of accomplishment or autonomy. This supportive feedback, woven through the daily interactions between child and caregiver, builds a foundation of trust and encouragement, a steady platform from which the child can leap into the world of problem-solving with confidence, knowing that each attempt, successful or not, is a step forward on their path to resilience.

In this exploration of building resilience through problem-solving skills, the journey unfolds as one of discovery, learning, and growth. From the initial steps of breaking down the problem-solving process to the dynamic rehearsals of role-play, from the empowering reframing of obstacles as opportunities to the nurturing touch of supportive feedback, each element contributes to the skillset of a child's development. This journey, marked by challenges and triumphs, shapes not just the child's ability to navigate the complexities of their world but also molds their character, embedding within them the seeds of resilience, empathy, and insight that will flourish throughout their lives.

CELEBRATING EMOTIONAL MILESTONES AND RESILIENCE

In the journey of emotional growth, moments that mark a child's successful navigation through the tumultuous seas of feelings and reactions stand as beacons of achievement. These milestones, often overlooked in the rush of daily life, deserve their spotlight, a celebration not just of the moment but of the journey it represents. Recognizing these milestones goes beyond mere acknowledgment; it's an affirmation of the child's resilience, a nod to the strength it takes to face and manage the whirlwind of emotions that comes with ADHD.

Recognition of Growth

Recognizing emotional growth requires a keen eye that sees beyond the immediate to the incremental steps that lead to mastery over a once insurmountable feeling or reaction. It's noticing when a child, who once would have been lost to frustration, takes a breath, steps back, and chooses a different path. These moments, small yet profound, are milestones worthy of recognition. They are the fruits of countless hours of practice, patience, and perseverance, both on the part of the child and those who guide them. Celebrating these achievements can be as simple as a verbal acknowledgment, a hug, or a shared moment of reflection on the progress made. It's a practice that bolsters the child's confidence and reinforces the value of their effort and the importance of emotional growth.

Resilience Stories

Stories have always been a medium for sharing wisdom, experiences, and lessons. In the context of fostering resilience, they become a powerful tool, weaving tales of perseverance, determination, and triumph over adversity. Sharing stories of resilience, whether from personal experiences, family history, or the lives of individuals the child admires, serves multiple purposes. It connects the child to a lineage of strength, showing them they are not alone in their struggles. It also provides concrete examples of resilience in action, offering inspiration and practical strategies for overcoming obstacles. These narratives, rich with emotion and triumph, paint a picture of resilience as an attainable, lived experience, encouraging the child to see their journey through a lens of possibility.

Emotional Achievement Awards

Creating a system of recognition for emotional milestones turns abstract concepts into tangible achievements. It could be an "Emotional Growth Chart," where milestones are plotted and celebrated, or "Resilience Ribbons," awarded for specific achievements like managing anger or speaking up about their feelings. This system, personalized to reflect the child's efforts and growth, is both a motivator and a visual reminder of their journey. It transforms the often invisible process of emotional development into something concrete, a collection of badges of honor that the child can look to as evidence of their strength and resilience. This approach validates the child's feelings and efforts. It instills a sense of pride and accomplishment, reinforcing the positive aspects of their emotional journey.

Family Rituals

Establishing family rituals around celebrating emotional milestones and resilience weaves the importance of emotional growth into the fabric of everyday life. These rituals, varying from family dinners where achievements are shared and applauded to monthly reflections on moments of growth and challenge, create a rhythm of recognition and celebration. They underscore the family's commitment to supporting each other's emotional journeys, highlighting the collective strength and understanding that binds them. These rituals become cherished practices, moments of connection, and mutual respect that highlight the significance of each individual's emotional growth and resilience.

A comprehensive approach to celebrating emotional milestones emerges in threading together the practices of recognizing growth, sharing resilience stories, creating a system for emotional achievement awards, and establishing family rituals. This approach acknowledges the complexity of the emotional landscape children with ADHD navigate, offering support, recognition, and celebration at every turn. These practices reinforce the importance of emotional resilience and foster an environment where feelings are validated, efforts are recognized, and achievements are celebrated.

As we close this exploration of celebrating emotional milestones and resilience, it becomes clear that these practices are not just about acknowledging achievements but about reinforcing the foundational skills of emotional intelligence and resilience that are vital for navigating life. They remind us that each step forward, no matter how small, is a victory in its own right, a testament to the child's courage, strength, and perseverance. It's a journey marked by its challenges and replete with moments of triumph and growth, each deserving of recognition and celebration. As we move forward, let us carry with us the lessons of this chapter, applying them in moments of achievement and everyday practices that shape our approach to emotional growth and resilience.

I recall a particular moment with my son that truly illustrated the power of celebrating small victories. He had been struggling with reading comprehension, often feeling frustrated and defeated. One evening, after weeks of patient practice and encouragement, he managed to read a short story without any help. The look of pride on his face was unforgettable. We made a big deal out of it, baking his favorite cookies together to celebrate. This wasn't just about the cookies; it was about reinforcing his perseverance and showing him that hard work pays off.

These moments of recognition are crucial. They serve as a reminder that progress is made up of many small steps, each one building on the last. It's about creating an environment where children feel safe to take risks, make mistakes, and learn from them without fear of judgment. This fosters a growth mindset, where challenges are seen as opportunities rather than setbacks.

In our daily lives, it's important to integrate these principles into our routines. When your child expresses a strong emotion, whether it's frustration over a difficult task or joy at mastering a new skill, take the time to acknowledge and validate those feelings. Use specific praise that focuses on the effort and strategies they used, rather than just the outcome. For example, saying, "I noticed how you took a deep breath and tried again when you were feeling frustrated. That was a great way to handle your emotions," reinforces the process of emotional regulation and resilience.

Furthermore, model these behaviors in your own actions. When you face a challenge, verbalize your thought process and coping strategies. If you make a mistake, own up to it and discuss how you plan to address it. This transparency not only humanizes you but also provides a practical example for your child to follow.

Incorporating family rituals that celebrate these emotional milestones can also be beneficial. Whether it's a weekly family meeting where everyone shares a personal achievement or a special dinner to mark a significant emotional breakthrough, these traditions can help cement the importance of resilience and emotional intelligence in your family culture.

As we move forward, let us carry these lessons with us, applying them not only in moments of achievement but also in the everyday practices that shape our approach to emotional growth and resilience. Remember, it's the consistent, small actions and recognitions that build a solid foundation for lifelong emotional health and resilience.

CHAPTER 8
POSITIVE DISCIPLINE AND THE ART OF REINFORCEMENT

Parenting a child with ADHD comes with its own set of challenges and wins, and discipline takes on a different role in this context. Instead of relying on outdated, punitive methods, discipline becomes more about growth, understanding, and positive reinforcement. In this chapter, we'll focus on the basics of positive reinforcement and how to use it in your daily life with your ADHD child. We'll cover topics like when to give rewards, balancing internal and external motivation, and how to create reward systems tailored to your child's unique interests. Let's get started and see how positive reinforcement can make a difference for your family.

UNDERSTANDING THE ROLE OF POSITIVE REINFORCEMENT

Principles of Positive Reinforcement

Positive reinforcement is about encouraging a desired behavior by giving a positive response right after that behavior happens. It's based on the idea that behaviors followed by positive outcomes are more likely to be repeated. For kids with ADHD, who often hear more about what they're doing wrong than right, positive reinforcement helps shift the focus to their successes. It creates an environment where they feel encouraged and supported, helping build their confidence and self-esteem.

To make positive reinforcement work, it's important to be specific about what behavior you're rewarding. Instead of just saying, "Good job," try something like, "I really liked how you finished your homework before playing your game." This helps your child understand exactly what they did well and encourages them to keep doing it. Also, consistency is key. Reinforce positive behaviors every time they happen, especially when you're starting out. Over time, you can gradually reduce the frequency of rewards as the behavior becomes more consistent. Remember, the reward doesn't always have to be something big—it could be extra playtime, a favorite activity, or just praise and recognition. The goal is to create a connection between positive behavior and positive outcomes, making it more likely your child will repeat those behaviors in the future.

Immediate vs. Delayed Rewards

The timing of rewards plays a critical role in the effectiveness of positive reinforcement. For children with ADHD, the immediacy of a reward significantly enhances its value, creating a transparent and tangible link between the behavior and its positive outcome. Consider a scenario where a child completes their homework without veering off task—an accomplishment, given the myriad distractions vying for their attention. Rewarding this focus with immediate praise or a small privilege reinforces the behavior at the moment, cementing the connection in the child's mind. In contrast, though valuable in teaching patience, delayed rewards often lose their immediacy, diluting the association between the behavior and its positive reinforcement.

Intrinsic vs. Extrinsic Motivation

While extrinsic rewards play a pivotal role in shaping behavior, fostering intrinsic motivation—the drive to engage in a behavior for its own sake—remains the ultimate goal. This internal motivation is nurtured by aligning rewards with the child's innate interests and passions. For a child fascinated by the stars, an evening spent stargazing can be an adequate reward for a week of completed assignments, merging their natural curiosity with the structure of positive reinforcement. This alignment bolsters the child's engagement and focus, cultivating a more profound, intrinsic love for learning and exploration.

To build intrinsic motivation, it's important to gradually shift from external rewards to experiences that are naturally rewarding for your child. Start by identifying what they enjoy or are curious about, and find ways to tie those interests into their goals. For example, if your child loves animals, completing their tasks could lead to a trip to the zoo or extra time learning about their favorite creatures. The idea is to help them see the value in the activity itself, not just the reward. Over time, as your child experiences the satisfaction of achieving goals tied to their passions, they'll begin to find motivation from within, reducing the need for constant external rewards.

Custom Reward Systems

Designing a reward system that resonates with a child's unique preferences and needs requires creativity, observation, and an open dialogue. This system, flexible and evolving, might include a variety of rewards, from tangible items like stickers or small toys to intangible ones such as extra playtime or a special outing. The key lies in customization, ensuring the rewards are meaningful and motivating for the child. For instance, a visual chart displaying a progression of tasks with corresponding rewards offers a clear structure, allowing the child to visualize their achievements and the rewards that await. This system serves as a motivational tool and a visual reminder of the child's progress, a tangible testament to their efforts and successes.

For example, when my son was struggling with staying focused during homework, we created a reward system that combined his love for building with LEGO sets. We set up a chart where he earned a small LEGO piece for every 15 minutes of focused work. Once he accumulated enough pieces, he could build something new with them. We even made the rewards more exciting by letting him pick out a larger LEGO kit that he could gradually work towards by meeting weekly goals. This simple system transformed homework from a dreaded chore into a challenge he was excited to tackle. The key was aligning the reward with something he already loved, which kept him engaged and motivated to stay on track. Over time, the system helped him develop better focus and work.

Strategy Section: Creating Custom Reward Charts

Custom reward charts can be an effective tool for encouraging positive behaviors in children with ADHD. By involving your child in the creation process and tailoring the chart to their unique interests and goals, you can create a system that is both engaging and motivating. Below is a step-by-step guide for parents on how to design and implement a custom reward chart at home.

1. Get Your Materials Ready

- You can start with a downloadable template or create a chart from scratch using poster board, markers, and stickers.
- Choose a design that appeals to your child—something colorful and visually engaging, possibly

featuring their favorite characters, themes, or hobbies.

2. Set Clear and Achievable Goals

- Start by identifying a few key behaviors or tasks you want to encourage, such as completing homework, listening during family time, or staying on task during chores.
- Make sure the goals are specific, realistic, and broken down into manageable steps. For example, instead of "be good during homework," break it down into "start homework on time" or "stay focused for 15 minutes."

3. Choose Meaningful Rewards

- Work with your child to select rewards that truly motivate them. Rewards can range from small, tangible items (like stickers or a favorite snack) to more experiential rewards (like extra screen time or a trip to the park).
- Consider using both short-term rewards for daily achievements and long-term rewards for bigger goals. For example, earning enough stickers throughout the week could lead to a bigger prize on the weekend.

4. Design the Chart Together

- Involve your child in the design process. Let them help choose colors, stickers, or themes for the chart.

This involvement gives them ownership and makes them more invested in using the chart consistently.
- Create sections for each goal with space to track progress. You can use stickers, stamps, or drawings to mark achievements as they work toward their rewards.

5. Implement the Chart and Track Progress

- Introduce the chart as a daily routine. Go over it together each morning to set intentions for the day, and review it in the evening to track progress.
- Use praise and encouragement along the way. Positive reinforcement is most effective when paired with genuine praise that acknowledges the effort behind the achievement. For example, say, "I noticed how focused you were during your homework time today—great job!"

6. Adjust and Evolve the System

- As your child grows and their needs change, so should the reward chart. Don't be afraid to tweak goals, swap out rewards, or change the design to keep it fresh and engaging.
- Regularly review the chart with your child to see what's working and what might need adjustment. This reflection helps keep the system relevant and effective.

Tips for Success:

- **Be Consistent**: Consistency is key to the effectiveness of a reward chart. Stick to the routine and follow through on rewards to build trust and maintain motivation.
- **Celebrate Successes**: When your child reaches a milestone, celebrate together! This could be a small family celebration or simply taking time to reflect on how far they've come.
- **Keep it Positive**: Focus on what your child is doing right, rather than what they're struggling with. This helps build their confidence and reinforces positive behavior.

By creating a custom reward chart, you're not just setting up a system for better behavior—you're fostering a deeper connection with your child through collaboration and mutual understanding. This hands-on approach empowers your child by involving them in the process, reinforcing positive behaviors in a way that's fun, engaging, and tailored just for them.

SETTING BOUNDARIES AND EXPECTATIONS WITH EMPATHY

Setting boundaries and expectations for a child with ADHD requires a careful balance of clarity, consistency, empathy, and flexibility. It's important to respect your child's unique perspective while also guiding them toward responsible behavior. This isn't just about enforcing rules; it's about creating a mutual understanding between you and your child. By establishing clear guidelines together, you help them know what's expected while giving them space to learn and grow within those boundaries.

Clear Communication

The cornerstone of this framework is clear communication. It's more than just saying words; it's about weaving understanding into everyday interactions. For example, it involves explicitly stating boundaries and expectations and explaining why certain behaviors are encouraged while others are not. This clarity isn't just in what we say but also in what we show—using visual cues and reminders to make the expectations clear and understandable. Role-playing scenarios can also help, as they allow the child to actively engage with and internalize the boundaries set. This way, abstract concepts become tangible realities they can grasp and remember, making the whole process more meaningful and effective.

Consistency is Key

The key to effective boundary-setting is consistency. This means sticking to the established rules and expectations, giving your child a reliable guide for their behavior. Consistency acts as a compass, offering direction in moments of uncertainty, ensuring that your child encounters the same response to a given behavior no matter when or where it happens. This practice requires diligence and coordination among all caregivers, presenting a unified front that upholds the agreed-upon boundaries, reinforcing their validity and importance.

I remember a time when my son was struggling with understanding the rules about screen time. One evening, after a particularly tough day at school, he begged for extra time on his tablet. It was tempting to give in, but I knew that staying consistent was important. I gently reminded him of our rule: no screen time after dinner. He was upset, but I explained why we had this rule and suggested we play a board game together instead. Over time, he learned that our rules were steady and fair, which helped him feel more secure and understand the importance of boundaries. This consistency, though challenging at times, taught him that rules are there to help, not hinder, and that we were all in it together.

Empathetic Enforcement

At the heart of this approach lies empathetic enforcement, which seeks to understand and address the underlying needs or emotions driving the child's behavior. This empathy does not negate the necessity of discipline; rather, it enriches it, framing the enforcement of boundaries within a context of care and support. When a rule is broken, the response, while firm, is infused with an effort to understand the why, engaging the child in a reflective dialogue that seeks to uncover the root cause of the behavior. It's an approach that acknowledges the child's feelings and frustrations, validating them even as it guides the child toward more appropriate expressions or solutions. This empathy fosters a deeper bond between parent and child, building trust and openness that encourages the child to share their thoughts and feelings more freely, secure in the knowledge that they will be met with understanding.

I remember a time when my son came home from school in a terrible mood. He lashed out at his younger brother, breaking our rule about treating each other with kindness. Instead of immediately punishing him, I sat him down and asked about his day. Through his tears, he told me about a difficult situation at school where he felt humiliated in front of his classmates. Understanding his frustration, I empathized with his feelings but explained that hurting his brother wasn't the right way to handle those emotions. We talked about better ways to express his feelings and even role-played some scenarios. This approach not only calmed him down but also helped him understand why he reacted the way he did and how he could handle similar situations in the future. This empathetic enforcement not only reinforced the boundary but also made him feel heard and supported.

Adapting Expectations

The fluid nature of a child's development, especially one navigating the complexities of ADHD, necessitates an adaptive approach to expectations and a willingness to tailor them to the child's evolving capabilities and stress levels. This adaptability recognizes that what is achievable one day may not be the next. The child's capacity to meet expectations can fluctuate based on many factors, from sleep quality to sensory overload. It mandates a continuous dialogue, an ongoing assessment of the child's current state, and a readiness to adjust expectations accordingly, ensuring they remain realistic and attainable. This flexibility extends to the methods of enforcement and encouragement, adopting creative strategies that align with the child's present needs and abilities. It's a dynamic process that accommodates growth and change, fostering an environment where the child feels supported in their efforts and motivated to strive within the bounds of their current capacity.

In this nuanced landscape of boundary-setting and expectation management, parents and caregivers create a framework of guidance that is firm, flexible, clear, and empathetic, providing the child with a stable structure within which to navigate their world. This approach, grounded in a deep understanding of the child's needs and perspective, fosters a relationship characterized by mutual respect and cooperation, laying the groundwork for responsible behavior and emotional growth. Through clear communication, consistency, empathetic enforcement, and adaptive expectations, families create a nurturing environment that encourages the child to explore their boundaries safely, learn from their experiences, and develop the skills necessary for self-regulation and positive social interactions.

THE POWER OF NATURAL CONSEQUENCES

In parenting, especially when raising a child with ADHD, natural consequences can be a powerful teaching tool that's different from traditional punishment. This approach is based on the idea that actions naturally lead to outcomes, allowing children to learn through their own experiences. With gentle guidance from parents, kids begin to understand responsibility and how their choices impact the world around them. This approach helps them grasp the cause-and-effect relationship that's a big part of everyday life.

Understanding Natural Consequences

To comprehend the essence of natural consequences, one must first distinguish it from the notion of punishment, a concept often laden with the intent of correction through imposed discomfort. Natural consequences, by contrast, allow the outcome of actions to unfold organically, offering a reflection of the real-world repercussions without the addition of parental censure. For a child with ADHD who navigates a world where impulsivity might often lead to actions, this approach offers a mirror to the consequences of their choices, fostering an internal dialogue about decision-making. If, for instance, a child chooses to spend their afternoon in a whirlwind of play, neglecting their homework, the natural consequence might be a rushed, stressful evening trying to complete assignments or realizing that incomplete work leads to academic repercussions. Here, the result directly flows from the choice, a lesson delivered by life itself.

Teaching Responsibility

Natural consequences teach kids that their actions have real impact and that they are responsible for their own choices. This happens when children experience the results of their decisions, whether it's the satisfaction of completing a project well or losing a privilege because they didn't follow through on a responsibility. As parents, our role is to guide them, not enforce rules. We can do this by discussing possible outcomes ahead of time and talking about the lessons learned afterward. This helps kids understand that their actions matter and can affect not only their own lives but also those around them.

As kids start to experience these natural consequences, it's important to help them connect the dots. For example, if your child forgets their homework and loses points, it's an opportunity to talk about how being prepared can lead to better outcomes. On the flip side, if they put in the effort and see positive results, acknowledging that connection reinforces the value of hard work. The key is to have these conversations in a supportive way, focusing on learning rather than blame. Over time, this approach helps them internalize the idea that their choices lead to real-world results, giving them a stronger sense of ownership and encouraging better decision-making.

Guided Experience

While the journey through natural consequences offers invaluable learning opportunities, it necessitates a delicate balance, ensuring that the child is supported and safe as they navigate the outcomes of their choices. This support takes shape in thoughtful guidance, where parents discuss potential decisions and their likely outcomes with the child, offering insights without steering the decision-making process. It's a collaborative exploration of possibilities, where the child is encouraged to weigh their options, pondering the likely consequences of each. In situations where the natural outcome of a choice could lead to harm or undue distress, parents gently intervene, guiding the child toward reflection and reconsideration. This process ensures that the child learns from their experiences in a context of safety and understanding, their journey through natural consequences framed by a supportive backdrop that encourages growth and learning.

One afternoon, my son was dead set on wearing his favorite superhero costume to the park, even though it was sweltering outside. Instead of saying no outright (and bracing for a meltdown), I figured this could be one of those "teachable moments" all the parenting books talk about. We had a little chat about how wearing that thick, head-to-toe outfit might make him really hot and uncomfortable. But hey, I let him make the call. And of course, he was determined to be the neighborhood's sweatiest superhero.

Fast forward about an hour, and there he was—red-faced, sweaty, and dragging his cape in the dirt. We found a shady spot, and I couldn't help but ask how he was feeling. With a sweaty nod, he admitted he wasn't exactly feeling like the cool, crime-fighting hero he had envisioned. We talked about how sometimes thinking ahead can save us from situations like this, where our decisions come back to bite us.

It was a perfect example of natural consequences in action. Instead of me forcing the lesson on him, he got to experience it himself (with a little guidance and a lot of sweat). No lecture needed—just a gentle nudge toward understanding that choices have real effects, and maybe next time, a t-shirt would be a better crime-fighting outfit.

Safety and Limits

Applying natural consequences is underpinned by a commitment to safety and appropriateness, recognizing that while experience is an influential teacher, not all lessons should be learned the hard way. This principle dictates that while a child might experience the discomfort of being cold after refusing to wear a coat, they would not be allowed to face situations where their well-being is at significant risk. Similarly, the consequences must be developmentally appropriate, aligning with the child's ability to comprehend and learn from the experience. It's a delicate calibration, ensuring that the outcomes of choices serve as constructive lessons rather than punitive measures. This calibration requires an ongoing assessment of the child's emotional and cognitive development, tailoring the application of natural consequences to their evolving capacity to understand and grow from the experiences life offers.

Navigating natural consequences while parenting a child with ADHD is a valuable learning process. It's about teaching responsibility and cause-and-effect in a way that respects the child's independence while ensuring their safety. With this approach, children learn from the real-life outcomes of their choices rather than imposed rules. Parents play a key role in this process by providing support, offering guidance, and helping children reflect on what they've learned. This method allows kids to better understand how their actions affect themselves and those around them in a meaningful way.

CREATIVE SOLUTIONS FOR COMMON BEHAVIORAL CHALLENGES

In the labyrinth of parenting a child with ADHD, finding the right path through behavioral challenges often requires more than a map; it demands creativity, a deep understanding of the child's unique perspective, and a willingness to engage in a collaborative journey of discovery and solution-finding. This intricate and multifaceted process allows for the exploration of the root causes of behaviors, the fostering of creative problem-solving skills, and the development of collaborative solutions that empower the child and reinforce their sense of agency and self-worth.

Behavioral Analysis

Peeling back the layers of a child's challenging behavior to uncover the underlying causes necessitates a keen eye, patience, and an analytical mindset. This deep dive begins with attentive observation, noting when and where challenging behaviors most frequently occur and under what circumstances they tend to escalate or subside. Tools such as behavior diaries, kept by parents and educators, provide invaluable insights, charting patterns and triggers that might be later apparent. The analysis extends to the child's emotional state and environmental factors, considering everything from sensory sensitivities to transitions between activities, seeking to understand the behavior from the child's point of view. This comprehensive approach lays the groundwork for addressing behaviors at the surface level and at their very core, paving the way for more effective and meaningful interventions.

I remember a time when my son struggled particularly with transitions, especially when it was time to leave the playground. The joy and excitement he felt while playing made it incredibly difficult for him to stop and move on to the next activity. After several meltdowns, I decided to try using a timer as a visual and auditory cue to help him prepare for the transition. I would set the timer for ten minutes before we had to leave and give him a heads-up, explaining that when the timer went off, it would be time to go. At first, he resisted, but over time, the consistent use of the timer helped him understand and accept the transition more smoothly. He even started reminding me to set the timer when we arrived at the playground. This small tool became a powerful aid in managing his transitions, reducing his anxiety, and making our outings more enjoyable for both of us.

Creative Problem-Solving

Encouraging a child with ADHD to engage in creative problem-solving transforms obstacles into opportunities for growth and learning. This process involves brainstorming sessions where no idea is considered too outlandish, fostering an environment where the child feels free to express their thoughts and suggestions without fear of judgment. Techniques such as mind mapping can visually organize thoughts and ideas, making the problem-solving process more tangible. Role-playing different scenarios and solutions allows the child to experiment with various outcomes in a safe and supportive setting, further enhancing their ability to think creatively and critically about their challenges. This approach not only aids in finding solutions to behavioral difficulties but also strengthens the child's cognitive flexibility, an invaluable skill in navigating the complexities of ADHD.

Collaborative Solutions

In the quest for solutions to behavioral challenges, including the child in the process is paramount. This collaboration acknowledges the child's insights and experiences as valuable contributions, building a partnership based on respect and mutual understanding. Families can establish routines and strategies that the child feels invested in, increasing their motivation to adhere to agreed-upon solutions. For instance, if morning routines are a source of stress and conflict, sitting down with the child to co-create a visual schedule or checklist might provide structure and predictability, which would help to reduce anxiety and resistance.

This partnership extends to setting goals and rewards, ensuring they align with the child's interests and aspirations, and enhancing their commitment to overcoming behavioral challenges. Through collaboration, children learn that their voice matters, bolstering their confidence and reinforcing their role as active participants in their growth and development.

Case Studies: Creative Solutions to Behavioral Challenges

Real-life examples of creative solutions to behavioral challenges serve as beacons for parents navigating similar waters, offering inspiration and practical guidance. Here are a few case studies that highlight the power of creativity, understanding, and partnership in addressing the behavioral challenges of ADHD:

Case Study 1: Taming Impulsivity in the Classroom

Meet Jake—a bright, energetic kid who just couldn't sit still in class. He was constantly fidgeting, blurting out answers, and struggling to stay on track, which wasn't doing him or his classmates any favors. After a few too many "Jake, please wait your turn!" moments, his parents, teacher, and Jake himself got together to brainstorm. The winning idea? A small, discreet fidget tool that Jake could use during lessons. It gave him a way to channel his restless energy without distracting everyone else. Slowly but surely, Jake started staying on task longer and felt more in control. The best part? His confidence grew as he realized he could manage his impulses and still be himself in the classroom.

Case Study 2: Turning Homework Drama into Homework Zen

Sarah's homework routine was a total disaster—every night was a battle, with endless study sessions leading to meltdowns and plenty of frustration for everyone involved. Her parents knew something had to change, so they tried a new approach: short, timed work bursts followed by quick activity breaks. They sat down with Sarah and came up with a plan that mixed work and play, so she wasn't overwhelmed by hours of non-stop assignments. The results were like night and day. Not only did Sarah start getting more done, but her attitude toward homework totally shifted. What used to be a dreaded chore became a much more peaceful (and even somewhat productive) part of the day. No more shouting matches—just a system that worked for everyone.

Case Study 3: Taming the Morning Madness

Mornings in Alex's house used to be pure chaos. Getting out the door for school felt like a daily disaster—lost shoes, forgotten homework, and a whole lot of rushing around. Every morning was a scramble that left everyone stressed out and exhausted before the day even started. Clearly, something had to change.

That's when Alex's parents decided to try a new approach: a visual morning routine chart. They sat down with Alex and mapped out everything he needed to do, step by step, from brushing his teeth to packing his backpack. To make it more fun, they added some of his favorite stickers as rewards for getting each task done on time. The chart was colorful, straightforward, and something Alex could easily follow on his own.

The first few days were a bit bumpy, but soon enough, the routine started to click. Instead of constant reminders and nagging, Alex could check his chart, see what was next, and move through his morning with less fuss. The stickers were a big hit, and he loved earning them for staying on track. Over time, the morning routine became smoother and way less stressful for everyone. No more frantic rushing out the door—the visual chart turned mornings into something much more manageable, setting a positive tone for the whole day.

These case studies, drawn from the experiences of families, educators, and therapists, illuminate the path for others, demonstrating how thoughtful, individualized strategies can effectively address the behavioral challenges of ADHD.

These case studies offer just a glimpse into the variety of strategies that can be tailored to meet the unique needs of a child with ADHD. The key takeaway is that finding the right approach often involves brainstorming, experimenting, and adjusting until you discover what truly works for your child. It's important to stay flexible and open-minded, and to remember that it's okay to ask for help along the way. Whether it's seeking advice from teachers, therapists, or other parents, or simply trying out new ideas, customizing the approach to fit your child's specific challenges is essential. There's no one-size-fits-all solution, but with persistence and creativity, you can find effective strategies that make a real difference. And while these are just a few examples, resources and support are readily available—whether it's through books, support groups, or even a quick search online—to help you explore even more tools and techniques that could work for your family.

In addressing behavioral challenges, it's essential to find creative solutions that respect the child's individuality, encourage their involvement, and promote understanding and empathy. By thoroughly analyzing the context of behaviors and employing imaginative problem-solving strategies, we can effectively tackle these issues. Involving the child in this process empowers them, helping them feel more in control and understood. This comprehensive approach helps children with ADHD build resilience, self-esteem, and a sense of mastery over their behaviors and choices.

For example, my son used to really struggle with the transition from playtime to bedtime. Instead of just enforcing a strict bedtime routine, we decided to tackle the issue together. When he was younger, we talked about why bedtime was important and brainstormed ways to make the transition smoother. Ultimately, we came up with a visual bedtime chart that included fun stickers he could place as he completed each step. Honestly, the main reason this strategy worked so well was because he got to have a say in how we approached it, and he picked out stickers he was genuinely excited about. This interactive approach made the routine more engaging for him and gave him a real sense of accomplishment. Over time, bedtime became less of a struggle and more of a bonding experience, showing us how effective it can be when kids feel involved and excited about the solutions.

As we wrap up this exploration, it's clear that the journey doesn't end here. Instead, we're stepping forward with new ideas and strategies, knowing that each child is unique and that the key often lies in being flexible, creative, and collaborative. The insights we've gained are just the beginning, equipping us with the tools we need to keep growing, learning, and discovering what works best for our children and families.

CHAPTER 9
NURTURING THE SEED OF ACADEMIC SUCCESS IN THE ADHD CLASSROOM

Imagine a classroom that nurtures each child's unique learning needs, a place vibrant with diversity yet united in its goal to cultivate understanding and academic growth. Here, children with ADHD bloom, not despite their challenges but because these very challenges are acknowledged, respected, and adeptly met with tailored strategies and accommodations. This chapter explores how to create an ADHD-friendly classroom, not through wishful thinking but through deliberate, informed actions and collaborations that bridge the gap between home and school, ensuring every child finds their place in the sun.

COLLABORATING WITH TEACHERS FOR AN ADHD-FRIENDLY CLASSROOM

Building Partnerships

The cornerstone of fostering an enriching learning environment for a child with ADHD lies in the strength of the partnership between parents and educators. This alliance, rooted in mutual respect and a shared commitment to the child's well-being, transforms the classroom into a nurturing ground for academic and personal development. Initiating this partnership involves reaching out to teachers early in the school year and setting a tone of open communication and collaboration. A meeting, perhaps over a cup of coffee during a quiet hour before the school day begins, is the perfect setting to discuss the child's strengths, challenges, and nuances of ADHD, laying the groundwork for a cooperative relationship.

We've been incredibly fortunate to have amazing teachers on our journey with our son. One teacher, in particular, made a huge difference by regularly checking in with us and sharing both the successes and struggles she observed in the classroom. She introduced a simple daily report system that highlighted key areas of focus, which helped us stay informed and proactive. This constant communication allowed us to work together to adjust strategies and support our son's needs effectively. There was one instance where our son was struggling with transitions between activities. This teacher suggested using a visual schedule and a timer, which we also implemented at home. This consistency made a significant impact, helping him feel more secure and in control. The supportive and open relationship we have with his teachers has been instrumental in his progress, showing us the power of a strong parent-teacher partnership.

Communication Techniques

Effective communication with educators hinges on clarity, consistency, and a focus on solutions. Regular updates, shared via email or a dedicated communication app, keep teachers informed about the child's progress and any recent adjustments in their ADHD management strategies. Equally, inviting teachers to share observations and insights from the classroom provides parents with a holistic view of the child's academic journey, identifying areas of success and opportunities for further support. This two-way communication stream ensures all parties are aligned in their approach, facilitating a responsive and adaptive learning environment that caters to the child's evolving needs.

Classroom Accommodations

Although it first felt this way to me, requesting accommodations in the classroom need not be a daunting task. Armed with a clear understanding of the child's ADHD and how it impacts their learning, parents can advocate for specific adjustments that mitigate these challenges. Accommodations might include:

- Preferential seating away from distractions.
- Additional time for assignments and tests.
- The use of technology aids to enhance focus and organization.

- The option for standing desk or alternative chair (my son loved the rocking chair for reading or a wobble cushion for his desk)

Presenting these requests with a focus on how they benefit the child's learning and engagement encourages a positive response from educators, fostering an environment where the child's potential is not overshadowed by ADHD.

Teacher Resources

Empowering teachers with resources and information about ADHD equips them to better support a child's learning. This could involve sharing articles, books, or online resources that offer insights into ADHD and effective classroom strategies. Workshops and professional development sessions on ADHD, perhaps suggested during a PTA meeting, can further enhance teachers' understanding and skills, helping them adapt their methods to meet diverse student needs. We've been lucky to work with teachers who were already highly knowledgeable about ADHD and gave us helpful advice that we could apply at home. However, not every teacher may have that experience, so offering additional resources when needed can be really beneficial. Taking this proactive approach to collaboration shows a commitment to supporting the child's academic and personal growth in a well-rounded way.

Strategy Section: Creating an ADHD-Friendly Classroom

Supporting children with ADHD in the classroom requires intentional strategies that help them thrive academically and socially. By working together, parents and teachers can establish an environment that meets the unique needs of children with ADHD. Below is an example of a classroom checklist that outlines key accommodations and strategies that have proven effective in creating an ADHD-friendly learning environment.

ADHD-Friendly Classroom Checklist

1. Structured Routines and Schedules:

- **Daily Visual Schedule:** Post a clear and consistent daily schedule that the child can see and reference throughout the day.
- **Predictable Transitions:** Use visual or auditory cues (like timers or music) to signal upcoming transitions between activities.

2. Breaks for Movement and Sensory Needs:

- **Scheduled Movement Breaks:** Incorporate short, frequent breaks to allow for movement, such as stretching, walking, or using a fidget tool.
- **Flexible Seating Options:** Provide seating choices like wobble chairs, standing desks, or cushion seats that allow for movement while learning.

3. Clear and Concise Instructions:

- **Step-by-Step Directions:** Break tasks into smaller, manageable steps and provide instructions both verbally and in written or visual form.
- **Check for Understanding:** After giving instructions, ask the child to repeat back what they heard to ensure clarity.

4. Interactive and Engaging Learning Activities:

- **Hands-On Learning:** Incorporate activities that involve physical movement, group work, and interactive games to maintain engagement.
- **Incorporate Interests:** Integrate the child's interests into lessons or assignments to boost motivation and focus.

5. Positive Reinforcement and Motivation:

- **Reward System:** Implement a reward system where the child earns points or stickers for completing tasks, which can be exchanged for small rewards or privileges.
- **Frequent Praise:** Provide specific and immediate praise for positive behavior and effort to encourage continued success.

6. Personalized Accommodations:

- **Noise-Canceling Headphones:** Offer headphones during independent work time to help block out distractions.
- **Assignment Adjustments:** Allow for extra time, reduced workload, or alternative assignments if needed to match the child's pace and ability.

Implementing and Reviewing the Checklist

This checklist serves as a starting point and should be personalized based on the child's specific needs. Regular communication between parents and teachers is crucial for assessing what's working and what needs to be adjusted. As the child grows and their needs change, the strategies and accommodations can be fine-tuned to ensure continued success.

By incorporating these practical strategies into the classroom, teachers can create a supportive environment where children with ADHD feel understood, valued, and equipped to learn. The collaboration between home and school is key to this process, helping children thrive in a space designed with their unique needs in mind.

IEPS AND 504 PLANS: ADVOCACY AND IMPLEMENTATION

Understanding the intricate web of rights and protections afforded to students with ADHD under the Individuals with Disabilities Education Act (IDEA) and Section 504 of the Rehabilitation Act represents a vital first step for parents navigating the educational landscape. These legal frameworks, designed to level the playing field, offer a beacon of hope, ensuring that children with ADHD receive the accommodations necessary to thrive academically. Grasping the nuances of these protections not only empowers parents but also equips them with the foundational knowledge to advocate for their child's needs effectively.

Navigating the IEP (Individualized Education Program) process requires preparation, knowledge, and persistence. It starts with formally requesting an evaluation, which obligates the school to assess your child's needs. Preparing for the IEP meeting involves gathering important documentation like medical diagnoses, teacher observations, and examples of your child's work. These pieces help create a clear picture of your child's strengths and areas of need. During the IEP meeting, parents, teachers, and specialists come together to discuss and create a plan that supports your child's current challenges and plans for future needs. The goal is to work collaboratively to ensure your child receives the accommodations and services they need to thrive.

In contrast, developing a comprehensive 504 plan focuses on ensuring that students with ADHD have equal access to learning opportunities, embedding accommodations into the fabric of their daily educational experience. This plan, less formal than an IEP but equally binding, hinges on identifying the child's specific barriers and outlining practical solutions to mitigate these obstacles. Crafting an effective 504 plan entails meticulously analyzing the child's school day. In these pinpointing moments, ADHD symptoms might hinder their learning or participation during pivotal times of day. Solutions range from modified testing environments to note-taking assistance, each tailored to the child's specific challenges. The strength of a 504 plan lies in its flexibility, allowing for adjustments as the child's needs evolve.

The relationship with the primary teacher is critical in this process, as they are the frontline in implementing and adjusting the 504 plan's accommodations. Open lines of communication between parents and the teacher are essential to ensure that any changes in the child's needs are quickly addressed. Regular updates and discussions help create a cohesive approach, where both home and school environments support the child's learning journey. This collaborative effort not only enhances the effectiveness of the 504 plan but also builds a supportive network around the child, fostering an environment where they can thrive academically and personally.

Advocacy within the educational system is both an art and a science, requiring a blend of dynamic commitment and strategic negotiation. Effective advocacy techniques hinge on a deep understanding of academic policies and a parent's rights within this framework. With this knowledge, parents can engage in discussions with school personnel from a position of informed confidence. Establishing a collaborative tone from the outset encourages a partnership approach, where the child's best interests form the central focus of all dialogues. Keeping detailed records of all communications and meetings serves as both a tool for reflection and a safeguard, ensuring that agreed-upon accommodations are implemented and adjusted as needed.

In this complex interplay of rights, accommodations, and advocacy, parents find themselves not just as defenders of their child's educational access but as architects of an academic experience that recognizes and celebrates the unique capabilities of students with ADHD. Through the meticulous crafting of IEPs and 504 plans and the persistent, informed advocacy that brings these documents to life, parents lay the groundwork for an educational journey that transcends the limitations of ADHD, fostering an environment where every child has the opportunity to reach their full academic potential.

The support and structure provided by the 504 plan have significantly eased our journey with our son. I remember the first meeting with his teacher where we discussed the accommodations and strategies outlined in the plan. Seeing the teacher's commitment and understanding, my husband and I felt a wave of relief wash over us. Knowing that we were not alone in this journey and that our son had a team of caring professionals looking out for him calmed our nerves and gave us hope. This collaborative approach has not only supported our son's academic growth but also provided guidance in his social-emotional growth and has also provided us with a sense of stability and reassurance through a challenging time.

HOMEWORK STRATEGIES THAT WORK FOR ADHD

Crafting an environment conducive to focused study and instilling a regimen that acknowledges a child's fluctuating rhythms of attention demands an inventive approach, particularly for those with ADHD. The quest for effective homework strategies becomes not merely an exercise in academic discipline but a delicate calibration of space, time, and motivation tailored to meet the unique needs and challenges presented by ADHD.

Creating an Effective Homework Space

The initial step in this nuanced process involves the creation of a homework zone that is both free from distractions and rich in resources conducive to concentration. This space, ideally situated away from the household's main thoroughfares of activity, serves as a sanctuary of calm, designed to shield the child from the cacophony of external stimuli that so quickly fracture their focus. Within this zone, everything from the lighting to the organization of supplies is considered, ensuring that the child has at their disposal all they require within arm's reach, thus minimizing the need for disruptive movement. Personalization plays a key role here, allowing the child to have a say in the setup, which fosters a sense of ownership and pride in their study area and ensures that the space truly resonates with their learning style and preferences.

Homework Routines

Establishing a routine for homework that aligns with the child's natural energy fluctuations throughout the day is crucial. This routine, far from being a rigid schedule imposed upon the child, emerges from an attentive observation of their most productive periods. For some, this may be shortly after returning home from school. For others, later in the evening, after rest and play. Once identified, this prime time for concentration is gently structured into a daily ritual, punctuated by explicit starting rituals, such as tidying the desk or setting out materials needed, signaling to the child's brain that it is time to shift gears into study mode. Regular short breaks are woven into this fabric, providing the child with necessary pauses to stand, stretch, or engage in a brief physical activity, thus preventing the buildup of restlessness that often derails sustained mental effort.

Breaking Down Assignments

For a child with ADHD, a lengthy homework assignment can loom like an insurmountable mountain, its summit lost in the clouds of overwhelm. Tackling this challenge requires a strategy of division, breaking the assignment into a series of smaller, more manageable tasks. This process begins with a review of the assignment, during which the child, guided by a parent or tutor, outlines the steps required for completion. Each step is then allocated a specific timeframe, transforming the assignment from a daunting monolith into a sequence of achievable goals. As each segment is completed, a sense of progress is palpable, providing the child with concrete evidence of their advance toward the assignment's completion. This method aids in managing the child's workload, builds their executive functioning skills, and teaches them how to approach complex problems strategically.

Motivation and Rewards

The engine driving this entire endeavor is motivation, a force that, for children with ADHD, often requires external fuel in the form of rewards. The key to an effective reward system lies in its immediate relevance and the personal value it holds for the child. Small incentives, tied directly to completing each homework segment, offer immediate gratification and a tangible sense of achievement, propelling the child forward through their tasks. These rewards, varying from extra screen time to a favorite snack, are most effective when chosen by the child, ensuring their desirability. Larger rewards can be set as milestones for longer-term projects or particularly challenging assignments, serving as beacons that guide the child through the extended effort required. This system of incentives does more than merely coax the child through their homework; it instills in them a deeper understanding of the relationship between effort and reward, a lesson that extends far beyond the confines of academic work.

Managing ADHD can be challenging, but the strategies discussed above can help make homework more manageable and even turn it into a positive experience. By organizing the physical space, structuring time effectively, breaking tasks into smaller steps, and using motivation wisely, parents and educators can create an environment where children with ADHD can succeed. This approach not only helps them achieve academic goals but also builds their confidence and sense of control over their learning.

ENCOURAGING LIFELONG LEARNING AND CURIOSITY

In the education landscape, particularly for children adorned with the vibrant spectrum of ADHD, curiosity acts as a spark and an enduring flame, illuminating paths of knowledge and understanding that conventional methods might overlook. This intrinsic drive to explore and question the world forms the bedrock upon which lifelong learning is built, transforming every moment and interaction into an opportunity for discovery. Nurturing this curiosity requires a delicate blend of encouragement, guidance, and the freedom to wander the vast expanse of their interests, leading to a love of learning that transcends classroom walls and academic requirements.

Fostering an environment where curiosity thrives involves a mindful approach, recognizing the child's natural inclinations and questions as gateways to deeper learning. It's about creating spaces at home where questioning is encouraged, where every "why" is met not with impatience but with enthusiasm or further inquiry, guiding the child to seek answers in books, experiments, or discussions. This atmosphere, rich with possibilities, allows the child's curiosity to flourish, unencumbered by the fear of judgment or the pressure of correctness. It's about showing them that learning is not just about finding the correct answers but about the joy of the quest itself.

The world beyond the classroom offers a vast, untapped reservoir of learning opportunities, each day brimming with potential lessons in science, history, art, and more hidden in plain sight. For a child with ADHD, whose attention might flit from one interest to another, these everyday moments become invaluable teaching tools. A walk in the park transforms into a lesson in biology, observing flora and fauna; a trip to the grocery store becomes an exercise in mathematics and economics; and cooking together becomes a practical demonstration of chemistry and nutrition. These experiences, grounded in the tactile, the tangible, and the immediate, resonate deeply with children with ADHD, providing a concrete context that enhances understanding and retention.

In the realm of literature, reading for pleasure opens doors to worlds both known and imagined, offering solace, adventure, and the quiet thrill of discovery. Encouraging a child with ADHD to delve into books might seem daunting. Yet, the key lies in aligning their reading material with their passions and allowing them to set the pace. Graphic novels, interactive eBooks, and audiobooks offer alternative formats that better suit their learning style, making reading an engaging, rather than burdensome, activity. This freedom to explore literature in all its forms fosters not only a love of reading but also enhances vocabulary, comprehension, and empathy as they immerse themselves in the lives and adventures of characters from diverse backgrounds and experiences.

Leveraging a child's interests as a vehicle for learning represents a powerful strategy, turning passion into a powerful educational tool. Whether it's dinosaurs, space, fashion, or computers, each interest holds the potential to expand into broader academic and life skills. Projects and activities designed around these interests capture the child's attention and provide a platform for developing research, critical thinking, and problem-solving skills. For instance, building a model rocket might involve physics and engineering, designing a video game could introduce coding and storytelling, creating a fashion portfolio offers lessons in art, history, and culture.

By bridging the gap between personal interests and academic learning, these projects imbue the educational process with meaning and relevance, making learning an integral, enjoyable part of life.

In this exploration of fostering curiosity and a love of learning in children with ADHD, the journey reveals itself not as a straight path but as a rich, meandering exploration, where questions lead to discoveries, interests fuel passion, and learning becomes an integral part of the child's identity. By encouraging inquiry, embracing learning opportunities outside the traditional classroom, promoting reading for pleasure, and leveraging personal interests, parents and educators can light the way for children with ADHD, guiding them toward a lifetime of curiosity, growth, and the joy of discovery.

As we wrap up this chapter, it's clear that curiosity, lifelong learning, and following individual interests are key to helping children grow. Education is really about nurturing each child's unique potential and supporting them as they find their way. As we move on to the next chapter, we'll carry forward the strategies and insights we've discussed, always keeping in mind the diverse needs of our children and the different ways we can help them succeed and thrive in their learning journey.

CHAPTER 10
FOSTERING SOCIAL FLOURISHING FOR CHILDREN WITH ADHD

In a world full of social complexities, making and maintaining friendships can be tricky for kids with ADHD. It's not that they're not trying, but their approach might be a bit different from others. This is where parents can help, not by controlling every interaction, but by offering support and guidance to help their child find their own way of connecting with others.

COACHING YOUR CHILD ON FRIENDSHIP SKILLS

Basic Social Skills

The foundation of any strong friendship is built on social skills, like greeting others, making conversation, and understanding non-verbal cues. For kids with ADHD, learning these skills can take extra time and practice. It's not just about telling them what to do—it's about giving them chances to practice in real-life situations. Everyday moments, like going to the park or attending a family event, become opportunities to work on these skills naturally. The key is repetition and making sure these skills are reinforced in different settings.

For example, if your child struggles with starting conversations, you might role-play how to introduce themselves or ask a question. Then, during a playdate or at the playground, you can encourage them to try it out. Afterward, talk about what went well and what was challenging. Over time, with consistent practice and support, these interactions become more natural, helping your child feel more confident in social situations.

Role-Playing Scenarios

The family dinner table or with stuffed animals at bedtime can be great places for children to practice social skills through role-playing. Role-play allows children to explore how different social interactions might play out, like how to join in on a game or handle a disagreement with a friend. It's a way to prepare them for real-life situations while building their confidence. Practicing these scenarios at home helps kids develop skills like empathy, negotiation, and conflict resolution, which they can apply when they're with their peers.

For example, you might role-play a situation where your child wants to join a group of kids playing at recess. You can take turns being the one who's asking to join and the one who's already playing. This helps your child think through how to approach others and what to say. After practicing, you can discuss what felt more effortless and more challenging. Over time, these rehearsals make social situations feel less intimidating, giving your child a toolkit of responses when interacting with others.

Empathy and Sharing

Empathy is critical to building meaningful relationships, and helping kids with ADHD develop this skill takes more than just talking about feelings. Creating experiences that help them understand and connect with others is essential. Activities like volunteering or reading books about different life experiences can be great ways to do this. These activities allow kids to step into someone else's shoes and see things from a new perspective. They learn that empathy isn't just about sharing toys and offering kindness, support, and understanding to those around them.

For example, involve your child in a community service project like helping at a food bank. Before and after the experience, you can talk about what it might feel like to be in need and how helping others can make a difference. Reading stories together about characters from different backgrounds can also spark discussions about how others feel in certain situations. Over time, these experiences help kids understand empathy on a deeper level, teaching them how to connect with others more thoughtfully and compassionately.

Navigating Friendships

Friendships can be a mix of fun times, disagreements, and making up, which can sometimes be tricky for kids with ADHD to handle. Helping them learn how to build healthy friendships means teaching them what to look for in a good friend—someone who values their unique qualities and treats them with kindness and patience. It's also essential to help them develop the skills to deal with the ups and downs of friendships, like handling misunderstandings or growing apart as interests change. The key is keeping communication open, letting your child express their thoughts and feelings while you offer guidance that encourages them to make good choices for themselves and others.

For example, if your child comes home upset after a disagreement with a friend, take the time to listen to their side of the story without jumping in right away with advice. Once they've shared, you can ask questions that help them think about what happened and how they might want to handle it next time. You can also role-play different ways to approach the situation, allowing them to practice problem-solving in a supportive setting. Over time, these conversations help your child feel more confident in navigating the complexities of friendship, giving them the tools they need to build positive and lasting relationships.

Strategy Section: Friendship Skills Checklist for Parents and Kids

Building friendships can be challenging for children with ADHD, but with the right tools and guidance, they can develop the social skills needed to form meaningful relationships. Here is a simple, engaging list of friendship skills that parents can share with their child. These activities focus on understanding emotions, practicing social scenarios, and building confidence in social interactions.

1. Understanding Emotions

- **Identify Facial Expressions:** Look at pictures of different faces and discuss what emotions they show (e.g., happy, sad, angry, surprised). Practice matching these expressions to feelings.
- **How Do You Feel Today?** Make a habit of checking in each day and talking about what emotions you're feeling and why. This helps kids learn to recognize and express their own emotions.

2. Starting Conversations

- **Conversation Starters:** Practice greeting others, asking simple questions like "What's your favorite game?" or "How was your day?" Role-play these scenarios to build confidence.
- **Taking Turns Speaking:** Teach the importance of listening while others speak. Practice taking turns in conversations by discussing a topic you both enjoy.

3. Practicing Social Scenarios

- **Role-Playing Common Situations:** Act out everyday social situations, like joining a group activity, asking to play, or handling disagreements. Role-playing builds familiarity and reduces anxiety in real situations.
- **Problem Solving Together:** Discuss what to do when things don't go as planned in a friendship, like if someone says something hurtful or if there's a misunderstanding.

4. Building Empathy and Understanding

- **What Would You Do?** Present a scenario, like "What would you do if your friend feels left out?" and discuss different ways to respond with kindness and empathy.
- **Reading About Friendships:** Explore books or stories about friendships. After reading, talk about how the characters felt and how they solved their problems together.

5. Creating a Friendship Goals Chart

- **Set Friendship Goals:** Work together to set small, achievable goals, like saying "hi" to a new classmate or inviting a friend over. Track progress with stickers or check marks.
- **Celebrate Successes:** Recognize and celebrate each small win, like making a new friend or resolving a conflict calmly.

This list serves as a guide for parents and children to work on friendship skills together. By practicing these activities regularly, children with ADHD can feel more prepared and confident in their social interactions. The key is consistency, patience, and celebrating growth along the way as they navigate the world of friendships in their own unique way.

NAVIGATING PLAYDATES AND SOCIAL GATHERINGS

Playdates and social gatherings are more than just fun activities—they're opportunities for kids to practice critical social skills. For children with ADHD, these events can be both exciting and overwhelming because they involve navigating social cues, expectations, and interactions that may be tricky for them. That's why it's helpful for parents to provide some guidance and preparation before these events. By setting up clear expectations and offering support, parents can help their children feel more confident and better prepared to connect positively with their peers.

For example, before a playdate, you might discuss what activities they could do and role-play how to ask someone to join in a game or take turns. You can also talk through scenarios that might be challenging, like what to do if they start feeling frustrated or if a disagreement comes up. By walking through these situations in advance, kids better understand how to handle themselves when those challenges arise. After the playdate, taking a few minutes to reflect on what went well and what could be improved can reinforce those lessons and help your child feel more ready for the next social event.

Preparation for Social Events

The anticipation of social events can stir a whirlwind of emotions in a child with ADHD, from excitement to apprehension. Mitigating this emotional tumult calls for a strategy of preparation that extends beyond the logistics of time and place, delving into emotional and mental readiness. This preparation begins with a dialogue, a gentle probing into the child's feelings about the upcoming event, acknowledging their excitement while validating any underlying nervousness. From there, envisioning the event together, discussing who will be there, what might happen, and how it might feel, paves a mental pathway, reducing the unknowns that fuel anxiety. This visualization process, coupled with reassurance and the assurance that their feelings are understood and shared, equips the child with an emotional blueprint, making the upcoming social landscape feel more familiar and less daunting.

Setting Up for Success

Crafting playdates that play to the strengths and needs of a child with ADHD involves careful planning and flexibility. It starts with the selection of peers and companions who display similar interests and qualities of patience, understanding, and the ability to adapt to the fluid nature of play that might characterize interactions with a child with ADHD. The environment, too, plays a pivotal role, with settings chosen to accommodate the child's sensory preferences and energy levels, be it the quiet corner of a garden, the structured environment of a craft room, or the boundless space of a park or playground. Within this chosen space, activities are curated for their potential to engage without overwhelming, structured enough to provide direction but open-ended enough to allow for the ebb and flow of attention and interest. This delicate balance ensures that the playdate offers a scaffold upon which positive social interactions can build, creating experiences marked by success and satisfaction.

Social Scripts

For many kids with ADHD, the unpredictable nature of social interactions can feel overwhelming. Social scripts can be a helpful tool to guide them through everyday situations, offering a set of responses they can rely on. These scripts can cover everyday interactions like saying hello, asking to join a game, or politely declining an invitation. Practicing these scripts beforehand allows children to get comfortable responding in different social settings. It's not just about memorizing lines—it's about helping them understand when and how to use specific phrases, along with the right tone and body language.

For example, if your child often struggles with joining group activities, you can work together on a script that they can use, like, "Hi, can I play too?" This interactive process involves role-playing different responses they might get, such as a welcoming "Sure!" or a less enthusiastic "Maybe later," and practicing how they could react in each situation. By rehearsing these scenarios, your child builds up a toolkit of responses that they can draw on when they're actually in a social setting. This kind of preparation can boost their confidence, making social interactions feel less intimidating and more manageable.

Feedback and Reflection

After the playdate ends, taking a moment to reflect can be really valuable. This isn't about critiquing every detail but rather a casual chat to see what went well and what was tough. It's a chance to celebrate the good moments—your child's kindness, their sharing, or their courage to try something new. These are the moments that make us proud as parents and give us hope for their future. It's also an opportunity to talk about any challenges in a supportive way. The goal is to focus on effort and progress, helping your child see that social interactions are a learning experience, not a test they have to pass. This understanding and patience are key, emphasizing growth over perfection and helping your child build confidence in their social skills.

For example, if your child found it hard to wait their turn during a game, you might say, "I noticed you were really excited to play. It's great that you're so enthusiastic! Let's talk about how we can work on waiting patiently next time." You can brainstorm strategies together, like practicing deep breaths, using a quiet counting game while waiting, or finding a distraction to focus on. This approach helps your child see each playdate as an opportunity to learn and improve, making social situations less stressful and enjoyable. With consistent support, your child can gradually build the skills and confidence to successfully navigate friendships and social settings..

DEALING WITH BULLYING AND SOCIAL CHALLENGES

Childhood social interactions can sometimes present tough challenges, and bullying is one of the most difficult for any child, including those with ADHD. As a parent, it's essential to be a source of empathy, guidance, and steady support. The first step is recognizing the signs of bullying, which can appear differently. Pay attention to changes in mood, sudden reluctance to go to school, unexplained injuries, or missing belongings—these could all be signs that something is wrong. Staying connected and keeping an open line of communication with your child is vital; rather than jumping in immediately, giving your child the space to open up about their experiences when ready is essential. By listening without judgment or pressure, you create an environment of trust, setting the stage for working together to address the issue.

When your child is ready to talk, you can explore strategies to handle bullying. Whether practicing assertive responses, involving teachers, or simply validating their feelings, the goal is to help your child feel empowered and supported. It's also essential to involve school staff when necessary, ensuring a clear plan is in place for keeping your child safe. You can guide your child through consistent communication and a team approach through these challenges, helping them build resilience and confidence.

Building self-esteem in children, particularly those with ADHD who might already feel marginalized, is akin to constructing a fortress from the inside out, brick by brick. Each affirmation and moment of pride serves as a bastion against external negativity. Strategies to bolster self-worth intertwine with daily life, from highlighting their strengths in vivid detail to setting achievable goals that lead to genuine accomplishment. Integrating positive affirmations into a routine, allowing the child to see themselves through a lens of capability and potential, nurtures a growing sense of self. This foundation of confidence helps protect children from the impact of bullying by reinforcing their sense of self-worth and awareness of their strengths.

Conflict resolution skills give kids the tools they need to handle disagreements with others. Teaching these skills involves more than just talking about them—it's about practicing how to see different perspectives and find compromises. Role-playing can be really helpful here, as it allows kids to work through pretend conflicts that are similar to what they might face in real life. These exercises help kids learn to respond in a way that is respectful and focused on finding a peaceful solution. By practicing these skills, children learn how to stand up for themselves while also respecting the needs and boundaries of others, which is an important lesson that applies to many areas of life.

Seeking support from school officials and counselors becomes a necessary step when the weight of bullying and social challenges surpasses a child's ability to cope independently. This action, far from admitting defeat, represents an assertive move to marshal the resources and expertise that institutions can offer. Initiating this dialogue, parents can serve as advocates, ensuring the child's voice and experiences are heard and validated. Collaboration with teachers, counselors, and administrators to implement anti-bullying policies and create a supportive educational environment underscores the collective responsibility to safeguard all children's well-being. Moreover, connecting with external resources, such as support groups and professional counseling, offers additional layers of understanding and tools for both children and parents, reinforcing that they are not alone in this journey.

The path forward weaves through recognition, empowerment, education, and collaboration in addressing bullying and social challenges. It's a path marked by resilience, where each step and strategy employed contributes to a collection of experiences that shape a child's ability to stand firm in the face of adversity, to know their worth, and to navigate conflicts with grace and assertiveness. Though fraught with challenges, this journey is illuminated by moments of triumph and growth, revealing the strength and resilience inherent in every child, guiding them toward a future where they survive and thrive in the richness of social interconnection.

FOSTERING EMPATHY AND UNDERSTANDING IN SIBLINGS AND PEERS

Children with ADHD often interact with others in ways that may not always match the typical patterns of their siblings or peers. While this can lead to valuable learning and growth, it also brings challenges in building understanding and empathy. However, these differences offer opportunities to develop deeper connections based on respect, empathy, and appreciation for each person's unique experience. By focusing on these values, families and friends can create stronger, more supportive relationships.

Educating Siblings and Peers

The task of enlightening siblings and peers about ADHD transcends mere dissemination of facts; it invites them into a lived experience, offering a glimpse into the world as perceived by someone with ADHD. Engaging in this educational endeavor often begins with open discussions that aim to demystify ADHD, breaking down the science in a way that is both accessible and relatable. Utilizing stories and analogies that mirror daily experiences, the aim is to paint a vivid picture of the challenges faced by individuals with ADHD, from the constant hum of distraction to the Herculean effort required for tasks that might seem trivial to others. This knowledge-sharing serves as a bridge, narrowing the gap of understanding and paving the way for relationships grounded in empathy and mutual respect.

To build on this understanding, it's helpful to involve siblings and peers in activities that offer a hands-on sense of what living with ADHD can feel like. For example, you might create a game where they have to follow instructions while being purposefully distracted, simulating the constant interruptions someone with ADHD might experience. Another idea is to ask them to complete a simple task, like sorting cards, but with a time limit and unexpected distractions thrown in. These exercises can give siblings and peers a better grasp of how challenging everyday tasks can be for someone with ADHD, fostering more patience and empathy in their interactions.

It's also important to have ongoing conversations where siblings and peers are encouraged to ask questions and express their feelings. Understanding ADHD isn't just a one-time lesson—it's a continuous dialogue that evolves as everyone's understanding deepens. By consistently checking in, you help ensure that the knowledge gained translates into everyday actions, like offering support during frustrating moments or finding ways to include everyone in play despite differences in attention and focus. Through these combined efforts, the goal is to create a more supportive environment where everyone feels understood and valued.

Family Meetings

Regular family meetings emerge as a pivotal strategy in cultivating a nurturing household environment where every member feels seen, heard, and valued. These gatherings, marked by openness and inclusivity, offer a platform for each family member to voice their thoughts, concerns, and celebrations. Within this safe space, discussions about ADHD and its impact on family dynamics can unfold naturally, allowing siblings to express their feelings and experiences. This collective engagement fosters a sense of belonging and togetherness. It encourages the development of collective strategies to support one another. Through these dialogues, family members learn to navigate the complexities of ADHD as a unified front, embracing diversity and fostering an atmosphere of understanding and cooperation.

To make these family meetings even more effective, it's important to establish some ground rules, like taking turns speaking, actively listening, and approaching discussions with kindness and respect. For example, you can use a "talking stick" or another object that indicates who has the floor, helping kids practice patience and listening. Setting a regular schedule for these meetings, whether it's weekly or monthly, creates consistency and shows that everyone's input matters.

During these meetings, you can also introduce practical problem-solving exercises. If a sibling is feeling frustrated because the child with ADHD is having trouble staying focused during shared activities, the family can brainstorm solutions together. Maybe you all agree to shorter play sessions with built-in breaks or use a timer to help everyone stay on track. Including everyone in the decision-making process not only empowers kids to feel part of the solution but also reinforces the idea that family is a team. This approach ensures that challenges are met with empathy and understanding, while also celebrating each family member's unique contributions.

Peer Support Groups

For children with ADHD, the journey toward social integration and acceptance often benefits from the solidarity found within peer support groups. These groups, whether formal or informal, provide a sanctuary where individuals with similar experiences gather to share, learn, and support each other. Participation in such groups offers children with ADHD a sense of belonging, mitigating feelings of isolation by connecting them with peers who truly understand the nuances of their experiences. These interactions, rich in empathy and devoid of judgment, empower children to share their challenges and triumphs openly, fostering a sense of community and mutual support. Moreover, these groups serve as a fertile ground for developing social skills in a forgiving and encouraging setting, nurturing growth and confidence in social interactions.

In addition to the sense of belonging and understanding, peer support groups can also be a valuable place for children with ADHD to practice and refine specific social skills. These groups often include activities designed to help kids work on things like turn-taking, active listening, and managing emotions in a supportive environment. For example, a group might play games that encourage teamwork and communication, or participate in role-playing exercises to navigate common social scenarios. The relaxed atmosphere allows kids to make mistakes and learn from them without fear of judgment, boosting their confidence in social settings.

Parents can also benefit from these peer support groups by connecting with other families who share similar experiences. By engaging in these networks, parents can exchange tips, strategies, and resources that have worked for them, creating a broader support system. Additionally, informal gatherings outside of scheduled group meetings—like playdates or social outings—can further reinforce the bonds formed within the group, giving kids additional opportunities to practice social skills and build lasting friendships in a low-pressure environment.

Celebrating Differences

At the core of fostering empathy and understanding is the celebration of differences, acknowledging that diversity in abilities and experiences enriches human interaction. Initiating activities highlighting each child's unique strengths and talents, including those with ADHD, encourages a culture of appreciation and respect. From art exhibits that showcase individual creativity to talent shows where diverse skills are applauded, these events serve as vivid reminders of the beauty inherent in diversity. Engaging siblings, peers, and the broader community in these celebrations makes the message clear: differences are tolerated and celebrated, fostering an environment where every child, regardless of their challenges, feels valued and understood.

Navigating sibling and peer relationships within the context of ADHD unfolds as a collective endeavor enriched by efforts to educate, communicate, support, and celebrate. Through these intentional actions, families and communities weave a fabric of understanding and empathy, crafting an inclusive environment where every child, including those with ADHD, finds their place. By embracing diversity and fostering connections built on mutual respect and support, we lay the groundwork for relationships that thrive on the beautiful complexity of human experience.

I remember a heartfelt conversation I had with my two boys when they were very young. One day, as we sat together in the living room, I took the opportunity to explain how their brains functioned differently. I told them that neither of their ways of thinking was better than the other; they were just different. I highlighted that each of them had things they found easy and things they found challenging. My older son excelled at building intricate structures with his legos, showcasing his incredible spatial awareness. My younger son, on the other hand, had an exceptional talent for storytelling, weaving tales with vivid imagination. By openly discussing these differences and celebrating what each of them was naturally good at, I could see a shift in their understanding and acceptance of each other. This conversation not only helped them appreciate their unique strengths but also laid the foundation for mutual respect and empathy, fostering a more supportive and loving relationship between them.

As we close this exploration, we are reminded of the power of empathy, education, and celebrating our differences in enriching the lives of children with ADHD and those around them. These efforts, while centered on addressing the challenges posed by ADHD, reverberate far beyond, touching the essence of human connection and the collective journey toward understanding and acceptance. With these foundations laid, we turn our gaze to the horizons of independence and self-care, ready to embrace the next steps in fostering resilience and empowerment in children with ADHD.

CHAPTER 11
NURTURING INDEPENDENCE IN THE ADHD LANDSCAPE

Few tasks loom as significant in the vast expanse of parenting as preparing a child for the leap into independence. This challenge magnifies when viewed through the lens of ADHD, where the typical hallmarks of growing up—self-care, organization, and decision-making—often bear an added layer of complexity. It's akin to teaching someone to sail in unpredictable waters, where sudden gusts and shifting currents demand skill and resilience.

Within this context, the focus shifts from merely navigating these waters to equipping our children with the compasses, maps, and tools necessary for their journey. The aim is not to steer for them but to ensure that, when the time comes, they can set their sails confidently, guided by the lessons we've imparted and their intrinsic strengths.

LIFE SKILLS FOR INDEPENDENCE: AN ADHD PERSPECTIVE

Daily Living Skills

At the heart of independence lie the daily rhythms of self-care—those tasks and routines that frame our days, from the moment we rise to the setting of the sun. For a child with ADHD, mastering these skills requires explicit teaching and a breakdown of each task into its component steps, displayed visually in a step-by-step checklist affixed to the bathroom mirror. Here, tasks like brushing teeth, showering, and choosing an outfit for the day transform from daunting chores into manageable segments. The key lies in consistency, repetition, and patience, allowing these routines to slowly embed themselves into the fabric of daily life until they become as natural as breathing.

Organizational Skills

Organization extends beyond the confines of a tidy desk or an ordered schedule; it represents the scaffolding upon which independence rests. For our children, this might begin with keeping track of belongings—creating a designated space for keys, wallets, and essential documents. Visual aids play a crucial role here, as do digital apps designed to alert, remind, and track. Imagine a weekly planning session where the child and parent sit down with a calendar to plot the week ahead, discussing commitments, responsibilities, and how best to prepare for them. This practice, grounded in the tangible, offers a dual lesson in time management and prioritization, skills critical for the road ahead.

To make these organizational habits stick, consistency is key. Regularly scheduled check-ins can be incredibly helpful, such as a Sunday night routine where you and your child review their upcoming week together. During these sessions, you can break down larger tasks—like a school project—into smaller, manageable steps, assigning specific days for each part. For example, instead of telling your child to "work on the science project," you might plan out Monday for research, Tuesday for gathering supplies, and Wednesday for building the model. This level of detail not only makes tasks feel less overwhelming but also teaches your child how to prioritize and allocate time effectively.

It's also helpful to incorporate tools tailored to your child's strengths and preferences. If they're more visual, you could use color-coded calendars or sticky notes to highlight important tasks and deadlines. For kids who prefer digital tools, there are plenty of apps that offer reminders, to-do lists, and even timers that help with time management. You can also encourage them to create personalized routines for everyday activities, like packing their backpack the night before school or setting out their clothes for the next day. By making organization a regular practice and giving your child ownership over the process, you're helping them build the independence and confidence they'll need to navigate the complexities of daily life.

Decision Making

Decision-making stands as a pillar of independence, a testament to one's ability to weigh options, consider outcomes, and make choices that align with one's goals and values. Teaching this to a child with ADHD involves more than theoretical discussions; it demands real-world application. Start with small decisions with low stakes yet tangible outcomes, gradually increasing the complexity. The process here is as vital as the outcome, involving a dialogue that unpacks each decision, explores potential consequences, and reflects on the choice made. When applied consistently, this systematic approach cultivates the skill and the confidence to make decisions independently.

To make decision-making more practical and engaging for children with ADHD, start by involving them in everyday choices that matter to them. For example, you can let them choose between two different after-school activities, decide what to wear for the day, or pick what the family will have for dinner. After they make a choice, discuss how it turned out—what went well and what could have been done differently. This reflection helps them see the connection between decisions and consequences in a real-world context.

As your child becomes more comfortable with smaller decisions, gradually introduce more complex scenarios. For instance, if they're saving up their allowance, you can guide them through weighing the pros and cons of spending versus saving for something bigger. You can discuss the potential outcomes and help them think through the longer-term effects of their choice. Over time, this approach not only builds decision-making skills but also reinforces the idea that every choice has an impact, fostering a sense of responsibility and independence.

Safety and Self-Advocacy

In the realm of independence, safety and self-advocacy emerge as critical components. These entwined threads run through the fabric of living independently. Teaching safety encompasses a broad spectrum, from physical well-being to digital security. It involves open, honest discussions about personal safety, understanding and respecting boundaries, and recognizing and responding to risky situations. Self-advocacy, meanwhile, embodies the ability to stand up for oneself, articulate needs and rights, and seek assistance when necessary. For a child with ADHD, these skills are honed through role-playing exercises, where scenarios ranging from seeking accommodations at school to navigating public transport are explored, dissected, and practiced.

Building on the foundation of safety and self-advocacy, it's important to offer real-life opportunities where your child can practice these skills. For instance, you might start by encouraging them to order their own food at a restaurant or ask a teacher for help with a class assignment. These small but significant experiences help your child build confidence in expressing their needs and asserting themselves in various situations.

Additionally, discussing safety in specific contexts is key. For example, you can have ongoing conversations about online safety, such as how to recognize scams, protect personal information, and respond to negative interactions on social media. You can also role-play situations like what to do if they feel uncomfortable in public, whether it's knowing how to ask for help or identifying safe spaces. Over time, these exercises not only reinforce the importance of safety and self-advocacy but also empower your child to feel more secure and independent in navigating the world around them.

TEACHING FINANCIAL RESPONSIBILITY AND PLANNING

Financial literacy is a crucial skill for navigating adulthood, helping young people manage the responsibilities of economic independence. Understanding how to handle money—like budgeting, saving, and spending wisely—requires more than just basic knowledge; it takes practice and self-discipline. For kids and teens with ADHD, who may struggle with impulsive spending, learning these skills early can make a big difference in their future financial stability. Teaching them how to manage their finances in a clear and practical way can set them up for success in handling money responsibly as they grow older.

Budgeting Basics

Learning how to budget is an essential first step in financial planning. Budgeting is about managing money by prioritizing needs, carefully considering wants, and setting aside savings for unexpected expenses. Creating their first budget for teens preparing for independence is a practical way to understand how money flows and what it takes to meet needs and wants.

Through activities like tracking expenses and planning for both small purchases and long-term goals, they get hands-on experience with managing finances. By regularly practicing budgeting, teens learn to make thoughtful decisions about their spending, balance their resources, and build good habits that help them achieve their financial goals.

Financial Tools

In today's world, technology plays a big role in teaching financial literacy. Digital tools and apps make managing money easier and more engaging, allowing users to create budgets, track expenses, and set savings goals. These platforms are especially helpful for visual learners, as they turn financial information into clear charts and graphs. For teens, including those with ADHD, these tools help make financial management more straightforward by providing reminders and visual cues that keep them on track with their goals.

For example, apps like EveryDollar or YNAB (You Need a Budget) allow users to link bank accounts, categorize spending, and set up alerts if they're overspending. A teenager could use these tools to plan how much they want to save for something specific, like a new game or a trip with friends, while tracking how close they are to their goal. Parents can also help by guiding their child through the process of setting up these apps, showing them how to use the features effectively, and checking in regularly to discuss progress. By incorporating these digital tools into their routine, teens can build practical financial habits that stick with them as they move toward greater independence.

Goal Setting

Setting financial goals is about transforming dreams into clear objectives, whether it's saving for something special, funding education, or planning a trip. For teens, it's crucial to start by defining specific, realistic goals and then breaking them down into manageable steps. This process instills patience and prioritization, helping them realize that it's often more rewarding to wait for something bigger down the line than to spend impulsively in the moment. By integrating these goals into their budget, they learn how to manage their current spending while keeping their long-term objectives in mind, giving them a sense of control over their finances.

For example, a teen might want to save up for a new gaming console. Together, you could help them set a target amount and determine how much they need to save each week. They might cut back on small, daily purchases—like snacks or extra app subscriptions—to put more money toward their goal. As they reach it, they'll see firsthand how setting a goal and sticking to a plan pays off. This experience builds financial discipline and shows them how to balance short-term desires with long-term goals, an essential skill for managing money effectively in the future.

Understanding Credit

Teaching teens about credit is crucial because it can either open doors or lead to financial trouble if not handled carefully. When introducing the concept of credit, it's essential to explain how it works, including the factors that affect credit scores, the benefits of good credit, and the risks of poor credit management. Teens should learn about the long-term impact of different credit decisions, like the consequences of carrying high-interest debt versus using credit strategically to build a solid financial foundation. Real-life examples, such as comparing the cost of paying off a loan with low and high interest, can make these concepts easier to grasp. Discussions should also cover loans, understanding interest rates and terms, and reading the fine print before signing anything. The goal is to help teens see credit not as a quick way to get what they want but as a tool that requires careful and responsible use.

For example, sit with your teen and walk through an introductory credit card statement together. Explain how interest accrues if the balance isn't paid in full and show them what happens when only the minimum payment is made monthly. You could also discuss how taking out a student loan works, what repayment looks like, and how making on-time payments can positively impact their credit score. By giving them this knowledge early on, they'll be better prepared to make smart credit decisions as they enter adulthood, helping them avoid common pitfalls and build a solid financial future.

SELF-CARE ROUTINES FOR TEENS WITH ADHD

Importance of Self-Care

Adolescence is a time of significant growth and change, where kids transition from childhood into adulthood. For teens with ADHD, self-care becomes an essential practice, not just a routine. Self-care includes habits that support physical and mental well-being, helping manage stress and emotions. When self-care is built into daily life, it helps create stability and resilience, giving teens the tools they need to handle challenges.

This could involve simple, consistent routines like getting enough sleep, eating balanced meals, and setting aside time for activities they enjoy. For example, you might help your teen establish a daily routine that includes time for homework, exercise, and relaxation. It's also important to teach them mindfulness practices, like deep breathing or short meditation sessions, which can help them stay grounded when they're feeling overwhelmed. Encouraging regular check-ins with themselves—asking how they're feeling and what they need—can make self-care a natural part of their day. These habits build a foundation of well-being that can support them both now and in the future, offering hope for a brighter, more resilient future.

Personal Hygiene Routines

Building consistent personal hygiene routines during adolescence is an essential part of self-care. These habits support physical health and help teens develop self-respect and confidence. For teens with ADHD, staying consistent with these routines can be challenging because they're easily distracted or overwhelmed. To help them stick with these routines, it's helpful to break tasks down into simple steps and create reminders that fit into their daily life. Placing visual cues in the bathroom or using checklists in their room can help keep these tasks on their radar. Additionally, choosing hygiene products they enjoy—like a favorite-scented shampoo or a fun toothbrush—can make the experience more enjoyable rather than feeling like a chore.

For example, if your teen struggles with remembering to brush their teeth twice a day, a checklist on the bathroom mirror or setting reminders on their phone can be practical. You can also work with them to establish an achievable morning and evening routine. Start small by focusing on just a couple of tasks—like brushing your teeth and washing your face—and build from there. Once these habits are established, they'll likely feel more confident caring for themselves, contributing to a sense of independence and personal responsibility.

Stress Management

Adolescence can be a stressful time, and for teens with ADHD, those challenges can feel even more intense. Managing stress effectively requires more than just pushing through; it's about finding strategies that actually work. Exercise is one of the best ways to relieve stress, whether through team sports, running, dancing, or any other activity that gets them moving. Physical activity helps release tension and boosts mood, making it easier to manage daily pressures. Mindfulness practices, like meditation, deep breathing, or even a quiet walk, can also be helpful. These techniques teach teens to stay grounded in the present moment and manage their emotions without getting overwhelmed. Finally, hobbies and creative outlets offer a break from stress, allowing teens to unwind and focus on something they enjoy.

For example, if your teen enjoys art, you can play a crucial role in encouraging them to set aside time each week to draw or paint. It can be a simple yet effective way to relax and express themselves. If they're into sports, your support in helping them find a regular activity they enjoy, like joining a local soccer team or going for evening runs, can make a significant difference. You can also introduce mindfulness gradually by doing short guided meditations together or practicing breathing exercises before bed. The key is to help your teen discover what works best for them so they can build a personalized toolkit for managing stress.

Healthy Relationships

Healthy relationships are an essential part of self-care, especially for teens with ADHD. However, forming and maintaining these connections can be challenging due to difficulties understanding social cues and managing emotions. Developing strong communication skills is critical. Teens must clearly express their needs, desires, and boundaries while learning to listen and understand others. Effective communication goes beyond talking; it's about genuinely listening and respecting different perspectives. Teens can build relationships based on mutual respect and understanding as they improve these skills. Setting boundaries is also crucial, helping them respectfully assert their needs and ensuring that their relationships are positive and supportive.

For example, you can practice communication skills at home by role-playing in everyday social situations. If your teen struggles with expressing their needs, you might rehearse a scenario where they politely but firmly say no to an uncomfortable request. You can also discuss the importance of active listening, where they practice repeating what someone has said to show they understand. Encouraging your teen to set personal boundaries—whether with friends, classmates, or even family members—helps them prioritize their well-being. Over time, these practices will help them build healthier, more balanced relationships that contribute positively to their growth and independence.

PREPARING FOR COLLEGE AND CAREER: BUILDING A SUPPORTIVE TRANSITION

Transitioning from high school to college or entering the workforce can be challenging, especially for individuals with ADHD. This time involves major changes and important decisions that require careful planning and support. It's essential to approach this transition in a way that considers the individual's specific needs while helping them build confidence and independence.

One effective strategy is to start planning early by breaking down the process into manageable steps. For example, if college is the goal, you can begin by researching schools that offer strong support services for students with ADHD. Visiting campuses, discussing available accommodations, and exploring time management tools can make a big difference in easing the transition. If entering the workforce is the focus, you can help your teen explore career paths that align with their strengths and interests. Practicing job interview skills, creating a structured daily routine, and finding strategies to stay organized at work are also key steps. By taking small, intentional steps and seeking out resources, individuals with ADHD can transition smoothly and confidently into this next phase of life.

Exploring Interests and Careers

Helping your child explore their interests and potential career paths requires a mix of encouragement and practical guidance. Providing opportunities to dive into their passions, like internships, volunteer work, or job shadowing, gives them real-world experience and a better understanding of different careers. These hands-on experiences can confirm their interests or even spark new ones, giving them more confidence to decide about their future. Open conversations about their goals and asking questions beyond surface-level interests help them think more deeply about what they truly want.

For example, suppose your child is interested in technology. In that case, encourage them to attend a coding workshop or volunteer at a local tech event. Afterward, discuss what they liked or didn't like about the experience. If they're unsure about their interests, you can explore options together, like career assessment tools or informational interviews with professionals in fields they're curious about. The goal is to give them enough exposure and guidance so they can make informed choices while feeling supported in exploring what genuinely excites them.

College Preparation

Preparing for college, especially for students with ADHD, goes beyond academics. It involves getting ready emotionally, building organizational skills, and learning the basics of independent living. Start by helping your child research colleges that match their academic goals and offer vital support services for students with ADHD. This can include looking into resources like extended test time, note-taking assistance, and priority registration. Visiting campuses and asking about available accommodations are critical steps in narrowing down the best options. Once you have a list of potential colleges, staying organized is essential for the application process—keeping track of deadlines, letters of recommendation, and other necessary documents. It's also a good idea to encourage your child to disclose their ADHD in their application, as this can provide important context for their academic history and show their resilience.

As you move closer to making a decision, don't forget to contact the college's disability services office to apply for any necessary accommodations before the semester starts. This will ensure your child has the proper support from day one. For example, suppose your child benefits from having extra time on tests. In that case, confirming this accommodation early can reduce stress once classes begin. Additionally, you can work with your child to create a plan for managing their daily routine—things like keeping track of assignments, maintaining a consistent sleep schedule, and practicing self-advocacy skills. These steps can help your child feel more confident and better prepared as they transition to college.

Vocational Training

For some students, a fulfilling and well-paying career doesn't always require a traditional four-year college degree. Vocational training and apprenticeships offer practical, hands-on learning experiences that directly lead to careers in information technology, skilled trades, and culinary arts. These programs are typically shorter than a college degree and focus on teaching specific skills needed for the job. For individuals with ADHD, the active, real-world learning environment of vocational training can be a better fit than traditional classroom settings, which often focus heavily on lectures and theory. If your child thrives in environments where they can learn by doing, exploring these options can be a valuable step in planning their future.

Discuss their interests and strengths to help your child consider vocational training or apprenticeships. Research programs that align with their skills and learning preferences, and look for options that provide solid support services. For example, if your child is interested in becoming an electrician, you could explore apprenticeship programs that combine on-the-job training with classroom instruction. These programs teach practical skills and often lead directly to job placement. By focusing on your child's strengths and learning style, you can help them find a path that sets them up for success in a career that's both satisfying and suited to their unique needs.

Transition Supports

As your child approaches the threshold of independence, identifying and leveraging the support and resources available for transitioning to college or the workforce becomes a priority. For students heading to college, this might include connecting with on-campus student disability services to establish a plan for accommodations and exploring peer mentoring programs where upper-level students can offer guidance and support. For those entering the workforce, support may take the form of job coaching or vocational rehabilitation services that assist in finding suitable employment, developing workplace skills, and navigating the expectations of professional environments. Beyond institutional supports, online communities and forums can offer advice, encouragement, and a sense of connection to others navigating similar paths. Encouraging your child to build a support network by connecting with these resources fosters a sense of empowerment and belonging, reinforcing the notion that they are not alone in their journey.

As this chapter draws to a close, it's clear that the transition from adolescence to adulthood, particularly for those with ADHD, is less about a single leap and more about a series of deliberate steps. From exploring interests and potential careers to preparing for college or vocational training, each phase is marked by opportunities for growth, learning, and self-discovery. Through thoughtful guidance and support, parents can help their children navigate this transition, equipping them with the tools and confidence to embrace their futures with optimism and resilience. As we move forward, the focus shifts to cultivating resilience and empowerment, essential qualities that underpin the journey toward independence and self-reliance.

CHAPTER 12
NURTURING THE NURTURER: THE VITALITY OF PARENTAL SELF-CARE IN ADHD PARENTING

Imagine a scene at dawn, the world still calm and gray, a parent standing by the kitchen counter, coffee in hand, gazing out the window. This quiet moment, fleeting as it may be, is a sanctuary, a brief pause in the relentless pace of life that comes with raising a child with ADHD. In these silent minutes, the day's challenges have yet to unfold, the night's struggles have softened in memory, and there's a chance to breathe. It's in this breath, this deliberate inhale and exhale, that the essence of self-care begins. For parents navigating the complexities of ADHD parenting, these moments of respite are not mere luxuries; they are the bedrock of resilience, the source from which they draw strength to meet each day with patience, understanding, and unwavering support.

Self-Care Practices

In ADHD parenting, self-care is crucial for maintaining your well-being and the stability of your family. It's about taking care of your needs to better support your child. This can include basic things like eating well, getting enough sleep, staying active, and making time for activities that bring you joy, like reading or spending time outdoors. For example, setting aside 30 minutes daily to read a favorite book or take a walk can give you a much-needed break and help you recharge. These small acts of self-care are essential for keeping yourself balanced and capable of handling the demands of parenting.

Additionally, building self-care into your routine is essential to become a regular part of your life, not just something you turn to when you're feeling overwhelmed. You might set up a daily or weekly schedule that includes dedicated time for yourself. For instance, if you enjoy gardening, you could plan a few hours every weekend to focus solely on that activity. By consistently prioritizing self-care, you're taking care of yourself and setting a positive example for your child, showing them the importance of balancing responsibilities with activities that bring fulfillment and relaxation.

Setting Boundaries

Setting boundaries is about clearly defining your personal limits and protecting your time and energy. It's a crucial aspect of self-care, allowing you to say no without feeling guilty, especially when it's necessary to prioritize your well-being. This means being clear and consistent with family, friends, and work about what you can and can't take on. Open communication is key—letting others know your needs and the reasons behind your boundaries helps everyone understand and respect them.

For example, if you've decided that evenings are your time to unwind, communicate that clearly to those around you. You could say, "I'm unavailable after 7 PM because I need that time to relax and recharge." Sticking to this routine consistently will reinforce the boundary over time. You can also practice boundary-setting in more minor situations, like politely declining a last-minute request to take on extra work or saying no to social plans when you're feeling stretched thin. These small steps help build confidence in setting boundaries, making it easier to protect your time and prioritize what matters to you.

Mindfulness and Stress Reduction

Incorporating mindfulness and stress reduction techniques into daily life can be a practical way for parents to manage overwhelming feelings. Practices like meditation, deep breathing, or yoga offer quick ways to pause, refocus, and bring calm to stressful situations. These activities help you become more aware of your thoughts and emotions, giving you a moment to decide how to respond instead of reacting impulsively. Taking a few minutes daily to engage in these techniques can lower stress levels and help you handle parenting challenges with a more evident mindset.

For example, start your day with a quick 5-minute meditation or practice deep breathing exercises before bed to wind down. You can also try incorporating mindfulness into daily routines—like focusing on your breath while doing dishes or taking a brief moment of stillness during a busy day. By making these practices a regular part of your routine, you can build a habit of managing stress more effectively, leading to a more balanced and calm approach to everyday challenges.

Seeking Support

Seeking support is incredibly important and helps parents connect with a community that understands what they're going through. Support can come in different forms, like therapy sessions that provide professional guidance, or joining support groups where parents share tips and experiences. Connecting with other parents of kids with ADHD, whether in person or online, reminds you that you're not alone in facing these challenges. These connections offer practical advice, emotional support, and a place to feel understood and validated.

For example, you might join a local ADHD parent group that meets monthly to discuss different strategies for managing school routines, or you could participate in an online forum where parents exchange tips on everything from handling meltdowns to finding the right resources. Therapy is another option that can provide tailored strategies for both you and your child, helping you navigate specific challenges. Building these networks gives you access to resources, encouragement, and a sense of community that can make a big difference in your journey as a parent.

BUILDING YOUR SUPPORT NETWORK: FINDING YOUR TRIBE

When parenting a child with ADHD, connecting with others who understand your experience can be incredibly comforting and supportive. Finding a community of parents who are going through similar ups and downs can offer valuable advice, understanding, and a sense of belonging. These connections often turn into trusted relationships where you can share both challenges and successes without judgment. Building this kind of support network takes effort, but it's worth reaching out and finding others who truly get what you're dealing with.

For example, you can join local or online support groups specifically for parents of children with ADHD. These groups provide a space to share resources, exchange tips, and offer emotional support. You might find a group through your child's school, community center, or even social media. Attending regular meetups or participating in online discussions helps keep you connected and gives you access to different perspectives and solutions. Over time, these relationships can become a key part of your support system, making the challenges of parenting a child with ADHD feel more manageable and less isolating.

Community Resources

Finding a supportive community often starts with local resources like ADHD support groups and organizations. These groups provide helpful information and a chance to connect with others who understand what you're going through. Schools and pediatricians are great places to ask for recommendations on workshops, seminars, and local groups where you can learn and meet other parents facing similar challenges. Libraries also host events and offer resources that bring together families looking for support and understanding. By connecting with these local resources, you can build relationships with others who truly get it, helping you feel less alone.

For example, you might attend a monthly support group at a local community center where parents share tips and experiences. During these meetups, you can discuss practical strategies for managing school routines or behavioral challenges, and you might even make friends you can rely on for ongoing support. Schools sometimes host events or information sessions about ADHD, where you can meet other parents and professionals. Taking that first step to engage with these resources can lead to valuable connections and a sense of belonging that makes the challenges of ADHD parenting feel more manageable.

Online Communities

In today's world, the internet makes it easy to connect with other parents facing similar challenges, no matter where you live. Online forums, social media groups, and websites provide spaces to share advice, stories, and support. These digital communities allow you to find guidance and encouragement from people who understand your situation, even if they're miles away. However, choosing groups that focus on positive, constructive discussions and offer genuine support is essential. In these online spaces, whether you're seeking help late at night or need a place to vent, you can find people who truly get it and can offer valuable insights.

For example, Facebook groups dedicated to ADHD parenting are a popular choice, where members often share tips for managing routines or navigating school issues. You might also find specialized forums that provide resources and advice for more specific challenges, like handling ADHD alongside other learning differences. By engaging in these communities, you gain access to a wealth of knowledge and experience, along with the reassurance that you're not alone in your journey. Participating in discussions, asking questions, and offering your own experiences can turn these virtual connections into valuable sources of support and friendship, providing a sense of relief in the midst of the challenges.

Building Friendships

Within the larger community of parents and caregivers, there's a real chance to form meaningful friendships with those who truly understand the ups and downs of parenting a child with ADHD. These connections might start in formal settings, like support groups or school meetings. Still, they often grow stronger in casual environments—like grabbing coffee, meeting at the park, or chatting during playdates. As you get to know each other, these relationships become a vital source of support, offering comfort and laughter on tough days and sharing the victories on the good ones. These friendships remind you that even in the challenges of ADHD parenting, there are bright moments of connection and joy.

For example, you might meet a fellow parent at a school meeting and later decide to meet for coffee, where the conversation flows more freely. Over time, you find yourselves turning to each other for advice, venting when things get tough, and celebrating milestones together—like when your child finally masters a problematic task. These relationships offer a sense of camaraderie and understanding that can be hard to find elsewhere. Knowing someone going through similar experiences can make the journey feel less isolating and more hopeful.

Professional Support

While peer support is incredibly valuable, professional guidance from experts who specialize in ADHD can be just as important for parents. Working with psychologists, counselors, or ADHD coaches provides research-based strategies and personalized advice that can make a big difference. These professionals offer practical tools and an objective perspective that helps parents plan for both immediate needs and long-term goals. Their expertise complements the insights and experiences shared within the parent community, providing a well-rounded approach to supporting your child. Through this professional guidance, parents can gain a deeper understanding and feel more in control in helping their child thrive.

For example, an ADHD coach might work with you and your child to develop routines that improve focus and organization. A psychologist could offer therapy sessions that address behavior challenges or emotional regulation. By integrating these resources into your support network, you're equipping yourself with knowledge and strategies tailored to your child's needs. Building relationships with professionals who genuinely understand ADHD can provide guidance and reassurance as you navigate this journey.

ADVOCATING FOR YOUR CHILD IN HEALTHCARE AND EDUCATION

Navigating the healthcare and education systems can feel overwhelming for parents trying to secure the proper support and accommodations for their child with ADHD. It's easy to get frustrated between policies, professionals, and endless paperwork. However, the goal is not to approach this process with confrontation but collaboration. By working with teachers, counselors, and healthcare providers, you can build a team focused on helping your child succeed and access the resources they need.

For example, when setting up an Individualized Education Plan (IEP) or 504 Plan at school, it's helpful to approach the meeting with clear goals and a cooperative attitude. Before the meeting, gather input from your child's teachers, relevant evaluations, and observations at home. This way, you can work with the school team to create a plan that best fits your child's needs. The same goes for working with healthcare providers—regular communication and a willingness to ask questions help ensure that everyone is on the same page. By building positive relationships with professionals and staying organized, you're more likely to achieve the best possible outcome for your child, and this journey can lead to significant improvements in your child's life.

Effective Advocacy Techniques

Advocating for your child requires a balanced approach that combines knowledge and understanding. To start, it's essential to be well-informed about ADHD, how it affects your child, and the rights and resources available to support them. With this information, you can clearly and confidently express your child's needs, framing your requests as collaborative solutions that work for everyone involved. Keeping detailed records is also crucial—having documentation of medical appointments, educational assessments, and communications with professionals gives you a clear picture of your child's progress and provides solid evidence during discussions about accommodations. Additionally, effective advocacy involves actively listening to healthcare providers and educators. Understanding their perspectives and limitations can lead to better cooperation and more productive outcomes for your child.

For example, when attending an IEP meeting, you might bring a folder with notes from recent evaluations, a summary of your child's challenges and strengths, and examples of what has worked well at home. This preparation not only helps you communicate your child's needs clearly but also shows the team that you're committed to working together. By staying organized and open to dialogue, you create an environment where everyone's goal is aligned—helping your child thrive both academically and personally.

Navigating Healthcare Systems

Navigating the healthcare system to find the proper support for your child with ADHD can feel overwhelming. However, with persistence and a clear plan, it's possible to access the care your child needs. The first step is finding the right specialists—those who have specific experience with ADHD and understand how it affects different kids in unique ways. Getting appointments with these experts can take time and flexibility. Still, their guidance is crucial for managing your child's condition. It's also essential to fully understand your insurance coverage, including what services are covered and how to advocate for treatments that might be denied. This process often involves handling paperwork, filing appeals, and staying patient. Still, it can make a big difference in getting your child the support they need.

For example, when seeking a therapist or specialist, you might ask your child's pediatrician for recommendations and then check which providers are in-network with your insurance. Once you find a potential match, be prepared for possible waitlists and follow up regularly to secure an appointment. It's also helpful to keep detailed records of any insurance claims or appeals you submit, including dates and outcomes, so you can stay organized throughout the process. These steps allow you to build a well-equipped healthcare team to address your child's specific needs and challenges.

Educational Rights

Within the educational sphere, the rights of children with ADHD are enshrined in legislation, offering a framework through which parents can advocate for accommodations and support. Familiarity with these laws, such as the Individuals with Disabilities Education Act (IDEA) and Section 504 of the Rehabilitation Act, equips parents with the legal backing to request modifications that can transform the educational experience for their child. This might include tailored lesson plans, extended test times, or providing a quiet exam room. Activating these rights necessitates a proactive stance, initiating meetings with school officials to craft Individualized Education Programs (IEP) or 504 Plans that reflect the child's needs. In these meetings, clear communication, backed by documentation of the child's ADHD diagnosis and its impact on their learning, paves the way for understanding and action, ensuring that the educational environment adapts to the child, not the other way around.

Collaboration with Professionals

Navigating healthcare and education for a child with ADHD requires a team effort, where parents, healthcare providers, and educators work together to support the child's growth and well-being. Building solid and cooperative relationships with these professionals is critical. Approach each interaction with respect, a willingness to listen, and a shared focus on what's best for the child. For example, you might work closely with your child's pediatrician or psychiatrist to adjust treatment plans as your child's needs change. In school, regular communication with teachers and administrators is essential for staying on top of your child's progress, discussing challenges, and celebrating successes together. This ongoing collaboration helps ensure that everyone is on the same page and that your child receives consistent support across all areas of life.

For instance, you might set up a monthly check-in with your child's teacher to discuss how classroom strategies are working or how any recent changes in medication are affecting their behavior and focus. On the healthcare side, maintaining a relationship with your child's providers by attending regular appointments and sharing updates about what's happening at school or home can lead to more personalized care. By keeping these lines of communication open and engaging with each member of your child's support team, you create a unified approach that is adaptable to your child's evolving needs. This adaptability ensures they have the best chance to thrive in school and daily life, giving them the confidence to manage their needs effectively.

EMBRACING YOUR ROLE AS AN ADHD ADVOCATE: MAKING A DIFFERENCE

In today's world, raising awareness about ADHD and advocating for those affected by it is more important than ever. Advocates are crucial in educating the public, challenging stereotypes, and promoting understanding. Advocacy goes beyond just spreading awareness—it's about driving real change that improves the lives of individuals with ADHD and their families. This can involve activities like volunteering, engaging in legislative efforts, and sharing personal stories highlighting the everyday realities of living with ADHD. Whether speaking up at school meetings, participating in community events, or working with policymakers, advocacy efforts help create a more informed and supportive environment.

For instance, you could join local initiatives to advocate for improved educational resources or take part in online campaigns that seek to boost funding for ADHD research. Sharing your family's experiences can be particularly impactful—whether it's through social media, blogs, or public speaking engagements, personal stories are potent instruments for fostering empathy and understanding. By participating in these advocacy efforts, you help foster a culture where individuals with ADHD receive better support, are more widely accepted, and are provided with the opportunities they need to thrive.

Raising Awareness

The quest to raise awareness about ADHD transcends mere conversation; it is a deliberate action that plants seeds of understanding in fertile minds, fostering a culture where ADHD is not a label but a part of the human mosaic. This mission finds its voice in many venues, from local community centers where workshops demystify ADHD to social media platforms where infographics and stories reach a global audience. Engaging in public speaking, whether at school board meetings or community events, allows for disseminating knowledge, challenging stereotypes, and highlighting the strengths that individuals with ADHD bring to the table. Though varied in scope and scale, these efforts share a common goal: to shift the narrative from misunderstanding to empathy, from stigma to acceptance.

Beyond these initiatives, real change often begins at home and within local communities. Parents, educators, and advocates play a crucial role in spreading awareness by having honest conversations, sharing resources, and creating spaces where those with ADHD feel seen and valued. Schools can implement better support systems, like flexible learning plans and sensory-friendly classrooms, while parents can connect with others through support groups that swap practical advice and encouragement. On a larger scale, organizations and influencers dedicated to neurodiversity use their platforms to promote factual information and debunk common myths, making understanding ADHD more accessible to everyone. The key is consistent, straightforward education that makes ADHD less of a mystery and more of something people simply get.

Volunteering

Volunteering, offering time and skills to organizations dedicated to ADHD, is a personal commitment to the cause and a beacon for community involvement. Opportunities abound, from participating in fundraising events that support ADHD research to providing administrative support for non-profits that offer resources and counseling to families navigating ADHD. In lending a hand, volunteers contribute to these organizations' growth and reach and stand as pillars of support, embodying the spirit of community and shared responsibility. This participation enriches the volunteer's life, offering a sense of purpose and connection. It strengthens the fabric of the ADHD support network, ensuring it remains robust and responsive to the community's needs.

Legislative Advocacy

Beyond the immediacies of community engagement and support, legislative advocacy offers a pathway to enduring change, influencing policies that shape the educational and healthcare landscapes for individuals with ADHD. This advocacy involves a nuanced understanding of the legislative process, identifying key policymakers, and crafting messages that resonate with the heart and the mind. Writing letters, making calls, and meeting with legislators, parents, and advocates can articulate the needs of the ADHD community and advocate for increased funding for research, support services, and educational accommodations. This concerted effort, often in collaboration with larger advocacy groups, seeks to embed the needs and rights of individuals with ADHD into the legislative agenda, ensuring they receive the recognition and support they deserve.

Sharing Your Story

Perhaps the most potent tool in the advocacy arsenal is the personal narrative, stories of struggle, resilience, and triumph that resonate with individuals and communities alike. Sharing these stories, whether through blogs, podcasts, or public speaking engagements, offers a window into the lived experiences of those with ADHD, breaking down barriers of misunderstanding and fostering a deep, visceral connection with the audience. These narratives highlight the challenges faced and celebrate the achievements, underscoring the message that ADHD does not define an individual but is merely one aspect of their complex, vibrant self. In sharing these stories, advocates invite others into their world, building bridges of understanding and empathy that span the chasm of ignorance and prejudice.

When people and families affected by ADHD come together, they create a strong foundation of awareness, support, and change. Their advocacy, based on personal experiences and a genuine drive to make things better, has the power to shift how society views ADHD, influence policies, and improve everyday practices. The goal is a future where ADHD is fully recognized, understood, and supported in all parts of life.

As we wrap up, it's clear that ADHD advocacy is both personal and community-driven, shaped by a shared goal of creating a more understanding and supportive world for neurodiversity. Whether it's spreading awareness, volunteering, pushing for better laws, or sharing personal experiences, every step helps move things forward toward greater acceptance and change. These efforts build a story of resilience, empowerment, and ongoing progress, laying the groundwork for future advocacy.

HOW DID WE DO?
YOUR FEEDBACK CAN MAKE A DIFFERENCE

**Share Your Experience
(And Help Other Parents Like Us)**

"When we understand the neurodivergent mind, we don't just parent; we empower. If this book has guided you toward new breakthroughs, your review could be the lifeline another parent is searching for."

MEGAN HILL, PHD

You made it to the end—woohoo! I hope you're leaving with a few more tools, a little more confidence, and maybe even a few laughs along the way. Parenting isn't easy, especially with all the twists and turns that come with raising a child with ADHD, but you're here and you're doing it!

Now that you've reached the end, I'd love to hear how the book resonated with you. Your honest feedback doesn't just help me—it helps other parents find what they need in the midst of their own chaos.

I get it, life's busy and writing reviews isn't usually at the top of anyone's list, but taking a moment to share your thoughts could be exactly what another parent needs to decide, "This is the book for me." Your words could help:

- A parent feel more prepared and less stressed about their child's next meltdown.

- A caregiver discover strategies that actually fit their family's real-life chaos.
- Someone struggling to feel supported in a world that doesn't always get the ADHD journey.

If this book brought you some peace of mind or made you feel just a little more "seen," I'd be so grateful if you'd take a minute to leave a review. You can scan the QR code or use the link below to be directly taken to the review page:

Leave Your Review Here

Thanks for walking through this journey with me—it's been an honor to share this experience with you. Your story and your input could be just what another parent needs to feel a little more hopeful.

With gratitude,

Megan Hill, PhD

CONCLUSION

As we reach the end of this book, let's take a moment to look back at what we've covered together. We set out with the shared goal of finding positive parenting strategies, gaining a better understanding, and appreciating the unique strengths that children with ADHD bring. We've talked about the impact of empathy, how to create routines that are both structured and flexible, and the importance of advocacy in building an environment where every family member feels supported and valued.

Through chapters rich with strategies for empathetic communication, we've discussed how to craft a home life that balances the need for routine with the beautiful unpredictability of ADHD. We've delved into the art of fostering emotional intelligence and resilience, touched on the positive impact of discipline rooted in understanding, and underscored the significance of forging strong partnerships with educators who play a pivotal role in our children's lives.

I've shared with you the cornerstone of my journey—parental self-care. It's a reminder that to pour into our children's cups, we must first ensure that our reservoirs are replenished. We discussed the necessity of building your support network, a community of hearts and hands ready to hold you up when the going gets tough. And let's not forget the power of advocacy, of raising our voices not just for our children but with them, championing a world that appreciates their unique brilliance.

At its core, this book celebrates neurodiversity, a call to shift our perspective from viewing ADHD as a hurdle to recognizing it as a different but equally remarkable way of thinking and experiencing the world. It's about focusing on our children's talents, fostering those sparks of creativity, curiosity, and boundless energy into flames of passion and success.

As we've discussed, parenting isn't a static endeavor; it's a dynamic, ever-evolving journey that beckons us to remain learners, open, and adaptable to new information and strategies that can illuminate our paths forward. The science of ADHD is constantly advancing; with it, our understanding deepens, offering new tools and insights to guide us.

I invite you now, more than ever, to lean into the communities surrounding you and share your stories and the wisdom gleaned from your experiences. Your journey, your challenges, and your triumphs have the power to light the way for others navigating similar paths. Whether through social media, forums, or direct conversations, your voice is a beacon of hope and solidarity.

To every reader who has walked this path with me, thank you. Your commitment to understanding, supporting, and loving your child with ADHD is a testament to the incredible parenting journey. Know that you are not journeying alone. The love and hard work you pour into this role daily are seen, appreciated, and shared by many, including myself.

As we close this chapter, remember that the story continues with each day, each challenge, and each triumph. I am filled with hope and confidence in the knowledge that our children can and will thrive, painting the world with the vibrant colors of their unique perspectives. I encourage you to keep the conversation going and share your thoughts, experiences, and insights with me and the world. Your story is an invaluable part of this ongoing dialogue and a source of inspiration and learning for all of us.

With heartfelt gratitude and warm wishes for your journey ahead,

Megan Hill

REFERENCES

ADDitude. (n.d.). *ADHD and bullying: How to stop the embarrassment.* https://www.additudemag.com/slideshows/no-more-bullying-strategies-for-adhd-kids/

ADDitude. (n.d.). *Communication skills for kids with ADHD.* https://www.additudemag.com/communication-skills-for-kids-adhd/

ADDitude. (n.d.). *Life skills: Your ADHD teen can build independence & confidence.* https://www.additudemag.com/life-skills-adhd-kids-need-to-know/

ADDitude. (n.d.). *Organizing tips for children with ADHD.* https://www.additudemag.com/helping-adhd-students-get-organized-for-school/

ADDitude. (n.d.). *Setting boundaries with family: Holidays, relatives & ADHD.* https://www.additudemag.com/setting-boundaries-with-family-adhd/

ADDitude. (n.d.). *Sibling relationships and ADHD.* https://www.additudemag.com/sibling-relationships-adhd-families/

ADDitude. (n.d.). *The best work schedule for ADHD brains: Flexible or rigid?.* https://www.additudemag.com/work-schedule-adhd-adults/

ADDitude. (n.d.). *The science of reward and punishment.* https://www.additudemag.com/positive-reinforcement-reward-and-punishment-adhd/

Architectural Digest. (n.d.). *How to design an ADHD-friendly home.* https://www.architecturaldigest.com/reviews/home-improvement/design-an-adhd-friendly-home

Beyond Booksmart. (n.d.). *ADHD and emotional dysregulation: Signs & how to improve.* https://www.beyondbooksmart.com/executive-functioning-strategies-blog/adhd-emotional-dysregulation

Centers for Disease Control and Prevention. (n.d.). *Parent training in behavior management for ADHD.* https://www.cdc.gov/ncbddd/adhd/behavior-therapy.html

Centers for Disease Control and Prevention. (n.d.). *ADHD in the classroom.* https://www.cdc.gov/ncbddd/adhd/school-success.html

CHADD. (n.d.). *ADHD & stress: Information for parents.* https://chadd.org/adhd-and-covid-19-toolkit/adhd-stress-information-for-parents/

254 REFERENCES

CHADD. (n.d.). *Parenting a child with ADHD.* https://chadd.org/for-parents/overview/

CHADD. (n.d.). *Improving the lives of people affected by ADHD.* https://chadd.org/

Childhood 101. (n.d.). *Teaching feelings: 30+ emotional literacy activities & resources.* https://childhood101.com/managing-big-emotions-best-resources-to-use-with-kids/

Edutopia. (n.d.). *Positive, intentional supports for students with ADHD.* https://www.edutopia.org/article/supporting-students-adhd/

Gottman Institute. (n.d.). *An introduction to emotion coaching.* https://www.gottman.com/blog/an-introduction-to-emotion-coaching/

Hes Extraordinary. (n.d.). *How to help children with ADHD develop problem-solving skills.* https://hes-extraordinary.com/problem-solving-skills-adhd

Hes Extraordinary. (n.d.). *How to teach kids & teens with ADHD about money.* https://hes-extraordinary.com/teaching-kids-about-money

Homeschooling with Dyslexia. (n.d.). *Effective reward systems for kids and teens with ADHD.* https://homeschoolingwithdyslexia.com/reward-systems-kids-and-teens-adhd/

Kennedy, B. (2022). *Good inside: A guide to becoming the parent you want to be.* Harper Wave.

Mayo Clinic Health System. (n.d.). *Helping a child with ADHD develop social skills.* https://www.mayoclinichealthsystem.org/hometown-health/speaking-of-health/helping-a-child-with-adhd-develop-social-skills

NCBI. (n.d.). *Barriers and enablers of service access and utilization for children with ADHD.* https://www.ncbi.nlm.nih.gov/pmc/articles/PMC10838487/

NCBI. (n.d.). *Mindfulness meditation training for attention-deficit/hyperactivity disorder in adulthood.* https://www.ncbi.nlm.nih.gov/pmc/articles/PMC4403871/

NCBI. (n.d.). *Professionally successful adults with attention-deficit hyperactivity disorder.* https://www.ncbi.nlm.nih.gov/pmc/articles/PMC5619157/

NCBI. (n.d.). *Stigma in attention deficit hyperactivity disorder.* https://www.ncbi.nlm.nih.gov/pmc/articles/PMC3430836/

Psychology Today. (2022, October 10). *How play might improve childhood ADHD.* https://www.psychologytoday.com/us/blog/21st-century-childhood/202210/how-play-might-improve-childhood-adhd

Reset ADHD. (n.d.). *9 essential self-care tips for parents of kids with ADHD.* https://www.resetadhd.com/blog/self-care-adhd-snkd9

Scientific American. (n.d.). *The creativity of ADHD.* https://www.scientificamerican.com/article/the-creativity-of-adhd/

The Art Farms. (n.d.). *The importance of celebrating developmental milestones.* https://www.theartfarms.com/uncategorized/the-importance-of-celebrating-developmental-milestones/

The Childhood Collective. (2021, October 14). *Teach growth mindset to your child with ADHD (or any child).* https://thechildhoodcollective.com/2021/10/14/4-strategies-to-teach-growth-mindset-to-your-child-with-adhd-or-any-child/

The Gottman Institute. (n.d.). *An introduction to emotion coaching.* https://www.gottman.com/blog/an-introduction-to-emotion-coaching/

They Are The Future. (n.d.). *Self-care for children and teens with ADHD (Parent guide).* https://www.theyarethefuture.co.uk/self-care-adhd/

Today's Parent. (n.d.). *5 tips for helping your kid with ADHD have better playdates.* https://www.todaysparent.com/family/special-needs/tips-for-helping-your-kid-with-adhd-have-better-playdates/

Verywell Mind. (n.d.). *Why children with ADHD need structure and routines.* https://www.verywellmind.com/why-is-structure-important-for-kids-with-adhd-20747

Verywell Family. (n.d.). *Using natural consequences as a discipline strategy.* https://www.verywellfamily.com/natural-consequences-as-a-discipline-strategy-1094849

WebMD. (n.d.). *Assistive technology for children with ADHD.* https://www.webmd.com/add-adhd/childhood-adhd/assistive-technology-adhd

WebMD. (n.d.). *6 ways a child with ADHD can study better.* https://www.webmd.com/add-adhd/childhood-adhd/study-better